CARIBBEAN FOLK TALES AND LEGENDS

For
Eliot and Jason

Caribbean writing and art were born out of the breath of the people's collective awakening. The writers and artists articulated their people's dreams.

JAN CAREW

From a letter from Northwestern University, Evanston, Illinois, April 22nd, 1974.

Caribbean Folk Tales and Legends

by

ANDREW SALKEY

Published by Bogle-L'Ouverture Publications
141 Coldershaw Road, Ealing, London W13 9DU

SBN (cloth) 0 904521 16 8 ✓
SBN (paper) 0 904521 17 6

Printed at the Press of Villiers Publications Limited
Ingestre Road, London NW5

CONTENTS

Acknowledgements

Acknowledgements and thanks are due to the Authors for permission to publish their retold folk tales and presented legends, in this Anthology. Grateful acknowledgement is also made to the following for permitting material to be reprinted: the publishers of CONTACT and the author, Petronella Breinburg, for "Came Worship", retold by the same author; the editors and publishers of THE INDEPENDENCE ANTHOLOGY OF JAMAICAN LITERATURE and the author, Louise Bennett, for "Anancy and Sorrel", retold by the same author; and the publishers of THE PIONEER PRESS and the author, Louise Bennett, for "Anancy and Commonsense", retold by the same author.

INTRODUCTION

Folk tales, myths and legends often conceal more than they tell; it's our business, as either listeners or readers, to winkle out the hidden meanings, associations and suggestions, and then have the courage to say, "Yes, our hopes, fears and dreams have been experienced before, long, long before our time, and here, now, is the proof of how very early they were experienced and spoken about and handed down, but in other words and images and metaphors, in other places and by earlier people!"

I, personally, have always been a passionate consumer of everybody's folk tales, myths and legends. In my childhood, in Jamaica, which was very happy and more than adequately catered for with oral Jamaican and foreign literary imaginative literatures by my teachers and even more so by my family, I found that I still had to top up my already ample story-diet with unexpected pickings of my own, from old books and magazines. And always it was just what I wanted: that surprising tale of revenge from Greek antiquity, or that story of the long hoped-for intervention of the God of Anger from Hindu mythology, or that thrilling narrative of the confrontation between the stubborn buffalo hunter and the powerful, all-seeing Keeper of the Wind in an American Indian legend. I couldn't get enough. I later learned that most people are just as interested in that sort of material, but with time, seem to be seduced by other stories and forms of entertainment and information which promise a firmer contact with the so-called real world. Pity! For the abundance of reality, and in some instances, real-life actuality, lodged deep in the stories of the folk tradition that I have listened to or read, would certainly turn out to be just as true and even more convincing for them, if it were put side by side with the other stuff from the real world.

And that takes me home. The Caribbean is very rich in its story-telling folk tradition. "We can tell ol'-time story with the bes' from any part of the world!" a Jamaican friend of mine in London once told me.

I've tried to do just that for my readers, with this anthology of eleven folk tales and five legends. The selections have been retold and presented by ten Caribbean believers in and committed contributors to our richly complex and varied folk cultures.

You will notice that eight of the sixteen contributions come from Guyana, that remarkable "country of the mind", as John La Rose, the Trinidadian poet and publisher, has described it. Well, Guyana is like that, fortunately, enviably! For me, at any rate, it's the land of the greatest cultural assets in the Caribbean, the landscape over which the believing eye may, indeed, glimpse a "traveller swimming on dry land", as Wilson Harris, the Guyanese poet and novelist, said in a public lecture in 1970, in Georgetown, his home city.

And so, from Guyana, watch out for the very special menace of the old woman in Ralph Prince's *Ol Higue*; from Surinam, the spellbinding interpretation of death according to the Djukas in Petronella Breinburg's *After One Life*; from Jamaica, the origin of the release of commonsense to the world at large, after Anancy, the Spiderman, trickster of tricksters, is himself outwitted, in Louise Bennett's *Anancy and Commonsense*; and, again, from Guyana, the beautiful, haunting Amerindian legend of the entry of the gods into the real world, presented by Jan Carew, in his epic, *Children of the Sun*.

And there's more, much, much more, which I hope will delight, instruct, perplex and even transport you, as I was, when I first read them.

ANDREW SALKEY

Folk Tales

Ol Higue retold by Ralph Prince
The Water Woman and Her Lover retold by Ralph Prince
The Fairmaid Comb retold by Joyce Trotman
Buru Tiga Play Dead retold by Joyce Trotman
Came Worship retold by Petronella Breinburg
After One Life retold by Petronella Breinburg
Bre'r Toucooma in Trouble retold by Knolly La Fortune
The Children's Friend retold by Vishnu R. Gosine
The Talking Donkey retold by Vishnu R. Gosine
Anancy and Sorrel retold by Louise Bennett
Anancy and Commonsense retold by Louise Bennett

OL HIGUE
Ralph Prince
(Guyana)   Folk Tale

The most dreadful scourge of an ol higue in Guyana took place in Essequibo, over one hundred years ago. Only the very old people know the story. They heard it when they were very young, because when it happened, none of them had yet been born.

In the village, where it happened, there was an old woman named Becky Winter, who had practised obeah for many years. But lately, because she was becoming feeble, many people, for whom she had worked obeah, were refusing to pay her. When she asked them for the money, they replied with rude remarks and vile curses.

One night, several of them went to her house and abused her, and pelted the house with stones, and called her, "Devil Whip Becky", and other bad names. One of the stones crashed through a window and cut her on her forehead. As the blood flowed down her face, she made a vow: that for sheer spite, for bad mind, for naked revenge, she would become an ol higue.

"Ye-e-e-ss!" she hissed to herself, as she wiped the blood from her face. "Aaahll right! Ah gwine become a real ol higue, a terr-rrable, terr-rrable ol higue. Ah gwine suck de blood outa aahll de young pickney o' dem rascal wha' gat money fo' me an' won' pay me. Aaahll o' dem! Ye-e-e-ss! Ah gwine suck de blood clean outa dey body an' lef dem dry, dry, dry!"

And so, for seven days and seven nights, Becky prepared herself to become an ol higue. She was a witch, an obeah woman, a mother of darkness. She drew on her forbidden knowledge and hidden powers in a dark corner

11

of her old house, and at midnight, of the seventh day, Becky Winter became an ol higue.

Late the following night, she went shuffling slowly down the road on her first mission of revenge. She wore a black turban, and a black dress reaching right down to her ankles. On her feet were black slippers, and under the folds of her dress she concealed a calabash.

No one seeing her would have suspected she was up to something unusual, because she was often on the road, late at night, and always dressed from head to foot in black.

The home she decided to attack was that of Stella Kelly, the woman who owed her the most money. Some-one had set a *jumbie* on Stella, which plagued her for years, and it was she, Becky Winter, who had got rid of it for her. "Wutliss, ungrateful bitch!" muttered Becky, as she approached the house.

She stopped under a tree nearby and quietly uttered magic words and made mysterious signs with her hands and snake-like wriggles with her body. Instantly, her wrinkled skin rolled off her body into the calabash, and she became a ball of fire.

The flaming ball rose in the air and slinked through a crevice at the top of a window. Rapidly, silently, it entered the bedroom. It found the cot with the baby and quickly changed to a hideous-looking old woman without skin. She bit the baby with a special soft bite, and then like a vampire, she sucked, and sucked, and sucked, until the baby was dry, dry, dry, completely drained of all its blood. Then, she grinned her ugly, ol higue grin. Swiftly she changed back to a ball of fire, and even before it rose from the floor and flew outside, the baby was dead.

Under the tree, the ball of fire changed back instantly to old, wrinkled-skin Becky Winter. She, then, shuffled back slowly along the road to her old house, grinning with

fiendish joy at having got her first taste of revenge.

Early next morning, even before sunrise, it was all over the village that an ol higue had killed Stella Kelly's baby. The baby was found lifeless, pale and flabby, and on the floor between the cot and the window there were blood stains.

Two days later, the baby was buried, and the villagers mourned. Every woman with a baby was afraid that hers would be killed. A very wise old woman called all these mothers together and told them what to do to protect their babies from the ol higue.

And this is what she told them: "Firs' t'ing is to get some white chalk an' mark crosses all roun' you house, an' draw a coffin wid de same chalk 'pon de grung. De nex' t'ing is to leh de baby sleep in a blue nightgown, an' put some asafoetida near de cot. Den get some raw rice an' t'row plenty 'pon de floor inside de bedroom. When de ol higue meet de rice she gat to stop an' count every single grain, one by one, An' if she drop even one grain or mek jus' one mistake when she countin' dem, she gat to start countin' all over again. Da gwine gee alyou a chance fo ketch de bitch an' beat she an' kill she."

Most of the mothers did just what the wise old woman told them to do. But some of them laughed and said that was superstition, and they declared that there was no such thing as an ol higue.

Becky Winter heard about this and went out of her way and found out who the women were that had dared to say there were no ol higues. There were six of these women, and each one had a baby. These were the ones she would smite next with her visitations of death, all six on the same night.

And, so, one night, about a week after the funeral of Stella Kelly's baby, Becky went out on her most frightful mission of death. Her grinning teeth made their soft bites and her wicked, greedy lips and tongue sucked the six

babies dry of all their blood and left them dead.

"Six more dead and gone," said Becky to herself as she shuffled slowly along the road back to her old house, grinning in fiendish joy, gloating over her revenge.

Dead and gone was Sandra, eight months old, daughter of Marva Jacobs, for whom Becky had worked obeah to make John Jacobs marry her.

Dead and gone was Henry, ten months old, son of Agnes Benjamin, whose husband Becky's obeah had made secure in his job.

Dead and gone was little Gwendolyn, just one month old. A *jumbie* had been set on her mother, Gloria Benn, and Becky's obeah had got rid of it.

Dead and gone was Patricia, six months old. Her father, Vibert Spencer, had been sick for a long time. It was Becky's obeah that had driven out the evil spirit which had tormented him and made him sick for so long.

Dead and gone was tiny Gladstone, barely two weeks old. His father, Maurice George, had stolen money and had been charged with larceny. It was Becky's obeah that had saved him from jail.

Dead and gone was Cecil, nine months old, whose mother, Louisa Roach, had hired Becky to work obeah on one of her enemies. The obeah was so powerful that the victim died from a mysterious illness.

Those were the six children that Becky Winter, the ol higue, had sucked dry, all in that one terrible night. The next morning, the villagers were lost in grief. Shock gave way to weeping and wailing, and silent tears.

And everywhere was heard the cry, "Ol Higue!" Many villagers had seen the ball of fire flying from house to house late that night when the babies were killed. And in the bedroom of every house, where death had struck, there were blood stains. It was now clear, even to those who had at first disbelieved, that it was a real and terrible ol higue that had killed the children.

On the night after the funeral of the six babies, the village women got together to plan what action they could take to catch the ol higue. In talking about it, they learned that the ol higue had struck only at the homes of those mothers who had ignored the advice given by the wise, old woman. As they talked about this with the six women themselves, they discovered something that startled them: three of these women and the husbands of three others had been dealing with an obeah woman, whom they still owed money. And the name of the obeah woman was Becky Winter.

And that was how the village women learned that Becky Winter, the obeah woman, had turned ol higue and sucked the seven children dead in revenge. So they put their heads together, until late that night, and they worked out a plan to catch her, and kill her.

It went into action, the very next morning. Becky was walking down the back steps of her house, when she saw something that made her cringe in terror. There, on the ground, in her backyard, were drawings in white chalk, of seven small coffins. Her eyes bulged in fear.

And then, she heard the cry, "Ol Higue!" She looked and saw a woman standing by the yard fence. And then another woman appeared by the fence and cried, "Ol Higue!" And then another woman shouted, "Ol Higue!" And another, "Ol Higue!" And another, "Ol Higue!" And yet other women kept appearing from behind the fence, until the yard was full of them. Then, altogether they roared at Becky, "Ol Higue! Ol Higue!"

Becky hurried back up the steps into the house and locked the door. The women surrounded the house, each with a piece of white chalk in her hand. They marked the house all over with chalk: the walls, the doors, the windows, the steps, and even the pathways to the steps. Then they shouted, "Ol Higue! Come outside! Ol

16

Higue! Come outside!" A crowd gathered, in the road, in front of the house.

Becky remained quiet, and peered at them through crevices in the windows. If she stayed inside, they would say she was afraid to cross the chalk marks. If she went outside, she would not be able to cross them, and that would betray her. Her only way of escaping was to change into a ball of fire. But that she could do only at night. And it would be only for the night, because she would have to return to her skin. She was trapped.

So all she could do was to stay in the house. Throughout the day people banged on the doors and cried, "Ol Higue! Ol Higue!" Becky heard women lamenting about the babies she had killed, and angry voices cried out for revenge. They were so enraged that Becky expected them to break into the house and kill her.

Killing her was in their plans, but they were waiting until night came.

Meanwhile as Becky sweltered in the hot, closed-up house and listened to the taunts and threats, she realised that there was only one thing left for her to do. As soon as it became dark, she would change into her ball of fire, and in one final burst of revenge, every child she found unprotected in the village she would kill. She was old and ready to die, and she knew she would have to return to face the village women and be beaten to death.

But she did not know that, before the beating, they would have a surprise for her. And they did not know that, after the beating, she would have a shock for them.

Becky made the first move. As soon as the sun set, she went to a dark corner of the house and uttered the magic words and made the mysterious signs and snake-like wriggles. Then, suddenly, she changed into a ball of fire. Her skin remained in the room, rolled up in the calabash.

A gasp went up from the crowd as they saw the flaming ball fly fast and high from the house. They watched it, as it flew among the houses, sometimes above the trees. Sometimes, it hovered near a window and then darted to another, searching for an unprotected bedroom where the ol higue's grinning teeth and hungry lips and tongue could find a baby and suck its blood.

All night long, it searched and found none. Every house had its guard of chalk marks, at all the windows and doors and crevices; every baby was sleeping in a blue night-gown; and everywhere, there was asafoetida with its strong garlic smell.

After searching the village in vain, the ball of fire flew back to Becky's house. There was a swarm of people in the yard; and the house was full of women who had broken into it and were waiting for Becky, armed with sticks. They had Becky's lamp burning, so that she could see the large heap of raw rice they had set for her in the middle of the floor.

As soon as the flaming ball entered the house, it changed back quickly to Becky Winter. And, as soon as she opened her eyes and looked around, she saw danger. She saw the women with the sticks in their hands, and their eyes blazing with hatred. She saw the heap of rice on the floor. And her skin began to burn like fire; the women had rubbed it all over with pepper.

Groaning in agony from the burning in her peppered skin, she kept on crying out: "Skin, yuh na know me? Skin, yuh na know me? Skin, yuh na know me?"

And even while she was being tormented by her burning skin, she was shuffling towards the heap of rice, in the middle of the floor. For she was bound by the ancient curse on ol higues to count the grains, one by one.

Soon, she stood over the rice. Then, she bent down low and started counting the grains, one by one.

The women gathered in a ring around Becky and raised their sticks in the air. Then, at a given signal, they brought them crashing down on Becky, knocking her to the floor.

18

She howled. She yelled. She screamed.

The women kept on beating her with their sticks, now red with blood. They became roused to a frenzy, growing wild with rage as they cried, "Dead, ol higue, dead! Dead, ol higue, dead!" And they kept on lashing and whacking at what was now just a pulp, a bloody mass. Blood was, now, splattering on their hands, their faces, their clothes, and all over the floor.

Suddenly, the old woman gave a deafening scream. Her body convulsed with snake-like wriggles; she uttered strange cries and made mysterious signs. Then, the women noticed something queer that made their hair stand on end; what they were, now, beating was only Becky's blood-soaked skin.

"Oh, Gawd!" cried one of the women. "Oh Gawd! Look, over dere!" They looked towards where she was pointing and saw a ghastly sight that froze them in a chill of horror, a sight that instantly turned some of them crazy, and haunted the others with nightmares for the rest of their lives; it was a hideous mass of raw flesh in the shape of a woman, lying on the bed, dripping blood.

THE WATER WOMAN AND HER LOVER
Ralph Prince
(Guyana)   Folk Tale

It's an old Essequibo tale they used to tell in whispers.
But even as they whispered the tale, they were afraid the
wind might blow their whisperings into the river where
the water woman lives. They were afraid the water
woman might hear their whisperings and return to haunt
them as she had haunted her lover.

It's a strange story. Here it is from the beginning:
There was an old koker near Parika, through which
water passed to and from the Essequibo river, for drain-
age of the lands in the area. On moonlight nights a naked
woman was often seen sitting near the koker, with her
back to the road and her face to the river.
She was a fair-skinned woman, and she had long, black,
shiny hair rolling over her shoulders and down her back.
Below her waist she was like a fish. When the moon was
bright, especially at full-moon time, you could see her
sitting near the koker, combing her long, black, shiny
hair, and singing softly to herself. She always sang strange
songs, beautiful songs, songs with haunting melodies, in a
musical voice most sweet to hear.
You could see very dimly just a part of her face, a side
view. But if you stepped nearer to get a closer look she
would disappear. Without even turning her head to see
who was coming, she would plunge into the river with a
splash and vanish. They called her Water Mama.
People used to come from Salem, Parika, Tuschen,
Naamryck and other parts of the east bank of the Essequibo river to see this mysterious creature. They would

21

wait in the bush, near the koker, from early evening, and watch to see her rise from the river. But no matter how closely they watched, they would never see her, when she came from the water. For a long time, they would wait, and watch the koker, bathed in moonlight, with silvery water round it.

Then suddenly, as if she had sprung from nowhere, the water woman would appear sitting near the koker, completely naked, facing the river and combing her long, black hair, shining in the moonlight. And always she would sing those beautiful songs with haunting melodies, in that sweet, musical voice.

There was a strong belief among the villagers in the area that riches would come to anyone who found Water Mama's comb, or a lock of her hair. So they used to stay awake all night at the koker; and then early in the morning, even before the sun rose, they would search around where she had sat combing her hair. But they never found anything. Only the water that had drained off her body remained behind, and also a strong, fishy smell.

The old people said that after looking at Water Mama or searching near the koker for her hair and her comb, or listening to her songs, you were always left feeling haunted and afraid. They told stories of people found sleeping, as if in a trance, while walking away from the koker. They warned that if a man watched her too long, or searched for her hair and her comb too often, or became too enchanted by her singing, he would dream about her. And if the man loved her and she loved him, she would haunt him in his dreams. And that would be the end of him, they said, because she was a creature of the devil.

The old people also warned that if the water woman ever turned her face full towards you, you would be frightened to death because her face was sometimes ugly like that of a hideous beast, and sometimes it was a hollow, white skull.

These warnings did not frighten away the younger and more adventurous men from the villages around. They kept coming from near and far to gaze at Water Mama. After watching her and searching for her hair and her comb, and listening to her songs, they always had that haunted fearful feeling. And many mornings, even as they walked away from the koker, they slept, as in a trance. But still they returned night after night to stare in wonder at that strange, naked woman.

At last, something happened; it was something the old people had always said would happen: a man fell in love with the water woman. Some say he was from Salem. Some say he came from Naamryck. Others say he hailed from Parika, not far from the koker. Where he came from is not definitely known; but it is certain that he was a young man, tall and dark and big, with broad shoulders. His name was John, and they called him Big John because of his size.

When Big John had first heard of Water Mama he laughed and said she was a *jumbie*. But as time went by he heard so many strange things about her that he became curious. And so, one moonlight night, he went to the koker to look out for the water woman.

He had waited for nearly an hour, and watched the moonlight shining on the koker and on the river. His old doubts had returned and he was about to leave when he saw something strange, something that "mek he head rise", as the old folks say when telling the story. He saw a naked woman sitting near the koker. A moment before, he had seen no one there. Then suddenly, he saw this strange woman sitting in the moonlight and combing her long, black hair. It shone brightly in the moonlight. And as she combed her hair, she sang softly to herself in a sweet, musical voice. Big John did not know the song she

23

was singing, but the melody moved him in a marvellous way, stirring up a yearning in his heart for someone to love.

Fascinated by the woman's singing, Big John made a few steps towards her to see her more clearly. But suddenly she was gone. Without even turning her head around to look at him, she plunged into the river with a big splash and vanished. Where he had seen her sitting, there was a pool of water. And there arose a strong, fishy smell. A feeling of dread overcame him.

He then set out to get away from there. He tried to run but could only walk. And even as he began walking, his steps were slow and his eyes heavy with sleep. And that is the way he went home, walking and staggering, walking and sleeping, as in a trance, barely able to open his eyes, now and then, to see where he was going.

The next morning, when Big John awoke and remembered what he had seen and experienced the night before, he became afraid. He vowed never to go back to the koker to look at the water woman.

That same night, the moon rose, flooding the land in silver, glistening in the trees, sparkling on the river. He became enchanted. His thoughts turned to the riverside and the strange woman combing her long, black hair, and singing her sweet, haunting songs.

And so, later that night, he stood near the koker, waiting and watching for the water woman to arrive. Just like the night before, she appeared suddenly near the koker, combing her hair in the moonlight, and singing softly to herself. Big John stepped towards her but she plunged into the river and disappeared. And once again he had that feeling of dread, followed by drowsiness as he walked home.

This went on for several nights, with Big John becoming more and more fascinated as he watched the water woman combing her hair in the moonlight, and listened

24

to her melodious singing. After the third night, he no longer felt afraid, and he walked into the pool of water she left behind. Sometimes he waited until morning and searched around for locks of her hair and her comb, but never found them.

After a few months of this waiting and watching, Big John felt sad and lost. He had fallen in love with the water woman. But he could not get near to her, so he stopped going to the riverside to watch her.

When the moon had gone and the dark nights came back, he began to drop her from his mind. But in another month the moon returned, flooding the land in silver, gleaming in the trees, sparking on the river. He remembered the water woman, and he longed to see her combing her hair again, and hear her singing her songs again.

And on that very night, when the moon returned, he had a strange dream. He saw the water woman sitting near the koker, combing her long, black hair, shining in the moonlight. She sat with her back to the river and her face full towards him. Her face was not ugly, as they had said, nor was it a hollow skull. Instead, it was pretty like a picture, and as she combed her hair she smiled with him, enchanting him with her beauty. He stepped forward to get a closer look, but she did not move.

And so, at last, he saw her clearly, her long, black, shining hair, her bright eyes, her lovely face, her teeth sparkling with smiles, and her body below her waist tapered off like a fish. She was the prettiest creature he had ever seen.

She, then, began singing to him. She sang softly, a sad song with a melody that moved him, stirring in his heart a strong yearning for love. He had never heard the song before, nor could he understand the words. But the melody haunted him, and the music of the song, and the sweetness of her voice, and the tenderness in her eyes all carried a message of love to him.

25

He stretched out his hands to touch her, and she gave him her comb and said, "Take this to remember me by."

Then, she jumped into the river and disappeared.

When he woke up the next morning, he remembered the dream. He felt happy as he told his friends about what he had seen in the dream. But they were afraid for him, and they warned him:

"Is haunt she hauntin' you."

"She goin' mek you dream an' dream till you don' know wha' to do wid youself."

"When she ready, she goin' do wha' she like wid you."

"Big John, you better watch youself wid de water woman."

"De water woman goin' haunt you to de en'."

These warnings made Big John laugh, and he told them: "She can' do me anyt'ing in a dream. I forget 'bout de water woman long time."

But they warned him again:

"You forget 'bout de water woman, but she don' forget 'bout you."

"Is you start it when you watch she so much at de koker."

"Now you 'rouse she an' she want you. Da is de story now, she want you."

Big John laughed off these warnings and told them that nothing was going to happen to him as nothing could come from a dream.

But, later that day, he saw something peculiar. It made him shiver with dread. On the floor near his bed was a comb. He could not believe his eyes; it looked very much like the comb the water woman had given to him in the dream. He wondered how a comb he had seen in a dream could get into his room.

When he told his friends about finding the comb they said:

"Is bes' for you to go 'way from dis place."

"Is you start it when you watch she so much at de koker."

That night he had another dream. In this dream he saw the water woman sitting in the moonlight. He stepped even closer to her than before, and she smiled with him.

For the first time since he had seen her, she was not combing her hair, and she had no comb in her hand. She pulled out a few strands of her hair and gave them to him and said, "Keep these to remember me by." And he took them in his hands and smiled at her. In another instant, she was gone with a splash into the river.

The next morning, Big John woke up with a smile, as he remembered the dream. But as he sat up in the bed, he found himself with a few strands of hair in his hands. His eyes opened wide in amazement. It was only then he realised that he was getting caught in something unusual with the water woman.

And so, the dreams went on, night after night. They became like magnets drawing Big John to bed early every night, and holding him fast in sleep till morning. They no longer made him feel afraid when he woke up.

In one dream, the water woman gave him a conch shell. The next morning, he found a conch shell on the floor. In another dream she gave him a handful of sand. The next morning, he found sand on his bed and grains of sand in both hands. One night, he dreamt that he and the water woman played along the river bank, splashing each other with water. The next morning, he found his bed wet, and water splashed all over the room.

Big John told his friends about these dreams, and they warned him that the water woman had him under a dream-spell. They were right, for he kept on dreaming about her, night after night.

Then came his last dream. The water woman stood by the riverside, holding a large bundle to her bosom. She

27

smiled and said, "You have my comb and strands of my hair. I have given you other little gifts to remember me by. Tonight, I shall give you money to make you rich. If you keep it a secret, you will stay on earth and enjoy it. If you reveal the secret, you must come and stay with me and be my lover for ever."

She hurled the bundle to him, and then jumped into the river and was gone.

When Big John awoke the next morning, he found the floor of the room covered with tens of thousands of five-dollar bills, piled up high in great heaps. It took him several hours to gather them and count them. It was a vast fortune.

Big John was too excited to keep the news to himself about the dream and the fortune it had brought him. He went around the village and told some of his closest friends about it. When they went with him to his house and saw those great piles of money, their eyes bulged and their mouths opened wide in astonishment.

Then they made a wild scramble for it. They fought among themselves all that afternoon for the money. A few of them got away with small fortunes. Some ran away with their pockets heavy with notes. Others were left with notes that got torn up in the scrambling and fighting. Big John himself was beaten by the others and got nothing. They ran away and left him.

What happened to Big John after that no one knows.

Some say he dreamt again of the water woman that night and she took him away in the dream. Some say he went to the koker several nights to look for her but never found her, and so he drowned himself in the river.

Others say that the water woman sent her water people for him, and that they took him to live with her, in her home, at the bottom of the river.

But if you go down to the koker near Parika on any night of the full moon, you would see the water woman

29

sitting with her back to the road and her face to the river, combing her long, black, shiny hair in the moonlight, and softly singing sweet, beautiful songs in a musical voice. You would also see a tall, big man with broad shoulders standing close beside her.

THE FAIRMAID COMB
Joyce Trotman

(Guyana)   Folk Tale

Everybody in the village was proud of Mr. Wilkie, and long after he was dead, people still spoke about him as if he was still alive. He used to be the richest man there. He had a very large house, with a big garden, lots of animals, even a motor car. Nobody knew for sure how he got so rich but on a Saturday night, when the moon was full and people sat on their back steps, chewing sugar cane, or eating boiled crab and swapping stories, this is the tale they tell of how Mr. Wilkie got rich.

When Mr. Wilkie was a young man in his twenties, he lived in a little one-room house, all alone, by Bush Corner, as they used to call the dam. Then one night he had to go to the neighbouring village for a wake. His Aunt Jess had died. He didn't really like the old woman. She was mean and stingy and there was very little love lost between them. But he had to show his face or he'd have to answer too many questions afterwards.

So there he was at the dead-house, full of people eating and drinking, playing cards and cracking jokes, and singing all the usual wake hymns as loudly as their lungs would allow them. Some shouted and screamed, others groaned in low tones, all in an attempt to show their "grief" at the loss of the beloved one. "Hypocrites, the lot of them!" thought Wilkie, and as the din grew more intense, the more eager he was to leave.

He was a rather quiet man, and the noise and confusion got too much for him, so when he thought that no one was looking he slipped quietly out of the house, slid step by step along the dam that ran beside the wallaba

palings, crossed a bridge further up and took the road for home.

It was just after midnight and it was pitch dark, but he knew the way and he wasn't really afraid. The only trouble was that he had to pass a koker, and people said that at night when everyone was asleep and the moon had gone in, the fairmaids came out to sit on the koker to comb their long hair. Wilkie never really paid any attention to this but nevertheless when he neared the koker he slowed down. Surely there was someone or something there! His heart began to beat *bup! bup! bup!* He walked more slowly holding his breath. Suddenly he heard a sound, like when you tearin' fugi, a slight thud on the ground, and a *bujung!* in the water. Someone had let out a suck-teeth, thrown something away, and then jumped into the deep black water in a hurry.

At first, Wilkie didn't know what to do. He couldn't turn back; he couldn't go forward; he stood there, as if carpenter had nailed him to the ground. Meanwhile, his heart was beating *budup bup, budup bup, budup, budup bup.* Then he picked up courage and moved. His right foot kicked something, and when he picked up the object, he saw that it was a comb. He put it in his pocket, hurried home to his house, the perspiration still dripping from his forehead, ran up the few steps to his door and made for bed as quickly as he could.

Later, he put the comb under his mattress and next day went about his work as usual. But, at night, when he lay down to sleep, he heard a gentle knocking at the door. He sat up, and listened. A woman's voice was crying, "My comb! My comb! Please, Sir! My comb!" Wilkie didn't answer; he was too afraid. He played for time and soon he heard the *flip flap, flip flap* of her tail, slipping from one treader to the next. Then he knew who his visitor was: the fairmaid of the koker.

He was very puzzled, when, in the morning, he found

34

a huge pile of money outside his door. He quickly gathered up the lot, put it in a canister under his bed, and said nothing. He had never handled so much money in his life. For a long time, he sat thinking about the money in the canister, not really believing that it was there.

The following night, the same thing happened. His fair-maid visitor came crying for her comb. He was too frightened to answer, and sure enough, next morning, there was another huge pile of money outside his door. Wilkie collected it carefully, put it with the rest in the canister and sat thinking for a long time. He was glad for the money, but he wasn't greedy and he didn't want anything to do with Water People. Gossipers in the village would soon begin to talk and he couldn't face that. What was he to do!

At the other end of Bush Corner, Ma Bec lived in a little house by the pump. She was the village adviser. So, he went to see her. "Maanin,' Ma Bec", he called out. "Yu de home?"

"A who da caalin' mi su soon?" replied a cheerful, welcoming voice. And Ma Bec stood at the door. "Come, son; laang time awi na taak. We you bin aal dis time?"

"Ma Bec, mi gat someting fu awi taak".

'Come, mi baay, le mi hear wa yu gat fu tel mi. Yu know Ma Bec always gat time fu liss'n."

So Wilkie and Ma Bec sat on the steps and he told her all about the fairmaid and the comb and the money. Ma Bec listened carefully, and for a long time after Wilkie had finished speaking, remained silent, until he began to wonder if she was there, at all.

"Wa mi mus' du?" asked Wilkie. "Mi na want nutten fu du wid dese Water People; mi na wan greedy man, but mi kyan do wid di money; you know how ting baad."

Then Ma Bec answered ."Shi gwine come, again, tonight. Lef wan big basket outside, and when shi come

35

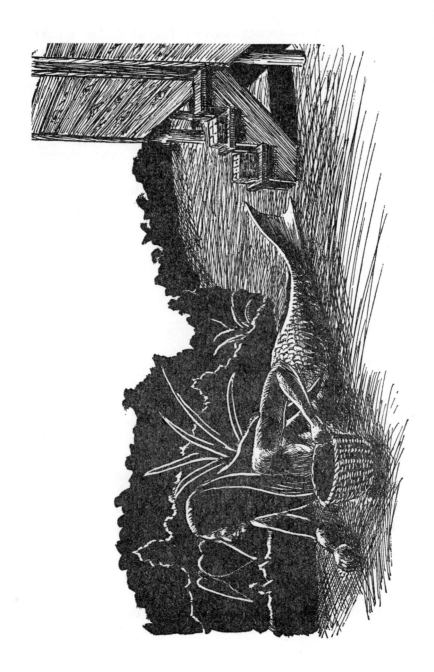

tell shi fu lef di money and tek di basket and gu an' bale out di sea. Yu na gu see shi no mo."

"T'ank you! T'ank you, Ma Bec!" said Wilkie, and hurried home to his house.

That same night just as Ma Bec said, the fairmaid turned up, crying all the time for the comb. At first Wilkie couldn't even talk, he was so afraid. Then as she continued to cry, he gathered up enough courage to shout at her. He told her to leave the money and to take the basket he had left outside, and bale out the sea with it.

He listened, his heart going *budup, budup,* all the time. The crying stopped; he was less tense. Then after a while he heard the *sl-i-i-ip slap, slip slap, sli-i-i-ip sl-a-a-ap* of her tail down the steps until the sound faded into the silence and the dark.

Wilkie didn't wait for day-clean. He got up quickly, collected the largest pile of money you ever did see, put it with the rest in the canister and lay awake for a long time, not even able to think straight.

In the morning, he opened the canister. The money was really there. It was real money, too. The first thing he did was to go to Ma Bec to report. He told her of the night's events and gave her some of the money. Ma Bec, once more, assured him that the fairmaid wouldn't return to molest him.

Very soon afterwards, people began to notice that Wilkie was wearing better clothes; he was building a bigger house on the public road; he was spending more money and he hadn't gone gold diggin' and come back. When anyone asked, he would show the comb, and then the old people would shake their heads knowingly. They understood.

So, on a moonlight night, on the back-steps, over boiled crab, or sugar cane, people in the village tell the tale of Mr. Wilkie and the fairmaid comb. And where is the comb? Buried somewhere in Mr. Wilkie's backyard. And where is the fairmaid? Still baling out the sea with a *mucru* basket.

BURU TIGA PLAY DEAD
Joyce Trotman

(Guyana)   Folk Tale

Buru Tiga sidding prapin' sarrow de 'hole maanin. Aal dem buru a laaf 'e 'caaze Nansi aalways mekin 'e look like a fool. Aal dis time 'e a taak to 'ese'f, "Mi gwine du fu dem; mi gwine du fu dem. Ha-ya!"

Den 'e git up, caal 'e wife and tell shi fu mek up a bed. She get nuff nuff dry pantain leaf and shi mek up a saaf saaf bed fu 'e. Den Tiga lay dung de, and tell shi fu halla haad an' tell every bady se 'e dead. Tiga lay dung, an' shut 'e yeye tight tight and' 'e wife staat fu halla. "O mi gaad! O mi gaad, ayu come quick! Ow! look mi hosban' come dead pan mi! O-o-o-w! wa mi gu du-u-u. O-o— ow! O mi gaado-o-o! Ayu co——m. Ol' house pan ol' house; cocobeh pan yaaz! O-o-ow! Ayu come na! Distress meet mi!'

Tiga wife cry su, an' aal dem buru hear and run come. Buru Daag, Buru Snake, Buru Goat, Buru Turtle, aal dem

39

buru. Some stan' up close; some stan' up far. De know se Tiga duz play smaat and de na know if 'e dead fu tru ar' if 'e a fool dem. Buru Snake cail 'e 'se'f caana wan pos but Buru Daag an' Buru Kyat gu mo' close 'caaze de kyan run.

Den aal dem buru staat fu halla an' cry an se how Tiga su good. 'Ow, awi gu miss Tiga! Ow, Tiga bin a wan good good compa!" Dis time, aal a dem know to de haat how Tiga baad. An' Tiga lay dung de, quiet quiet, 'e yeye shut tight, tight, an' 'e a hol' in 'e breat', and 'e wife de baalin' shi soul-case out.

Only Buru Goat na trus' Tiga. How Tiga kyan come dead dry dry su? E na sick nutten. But na min' dat, 'e baal like everybady, but 'e a liss'n and 'e a watch. Den 'e en gun hear Tiga fart? Man, mi tell you Tiga fiah wan big fart, but wid all di naise only goat hear, caaze 'e stan' up close.

Goat move way easy easy an' staat fu gu rung to dem buru wan bi wan, an' unda 'e breat' 'e a se, "Man dead; man a faat? Man dead; man a faat? Man dead; man a faat?" Eh! eh! wan, wan, dem buru, get quiet an' de staat fu slide way. Buru Snake slip in di bush; Buru Turtle pull 'e head inside 'e house; Buru Kyat mek a spring and disappear like fiah de pan 'e tail. All dem Buru gu crass di canal and stan' up pan di ada side. Only Buru Daag and Buru Goat lef.

Dis time Tiga lay dung de, waitin'. 'E open 'e yeye lil bit. "Eh! Eh! Nobody na de!" den 'e git up and when 'e see Goat 'e staat fu chase 'e. Now 'e know se a Goat trick 'e dis time.

Goat light out, wid Buru Daag gwine full but dung di dam, an' Tiga de behin'. Aal dem aada buru de crass di canal. Only Buru Daag and Buru Goat lef. But Goat kyaan run no mo, 'e lay dung pan di grass, caana di canal, wid 'e haarn lef stickin' out. Buru Daag ketch up wid 'e

40

and tel 'e jump. "Jump, Buru Goat! Look, Tiga comin'! Jump, nuh! Jump!" But po' Goat 'e so weary now, an 'e so friken, 'e kyaan move, an' Tiga de pan dem! So Buru Daag tek Goat by 'e haarn an' pitch 'e ova di canal an' den 'esef jump in de waata fas' fas' an' swim craas.

Betime Tiga meet, dem two de pan de aada ova, an' Buru Goat halla pan Tiga, "Me-e-h! Me-e-eh! Man dead; man a faat; Man dead; man a faat!" An' 'e and Daag bus wan big laaf an' de lef Tiga de, mo bex dan' befo' an' mo shame tu. So now awi duz se:

"Goat de crass waata, da mek 'e kyan gi Tiga saacy."

41

CAME WORSHIP
Petronella Breinburg
(Surinam)
Creole Folk Tale

For a very long time, Earth's creatures took everything for granted. The creatures ate, drank, enjoyed themselves, without stopping to think from where and how all the good things came. Without stopping to think or to give thanks, the creatures enjoyed the beauty of the earth they lived on; the flowers, the trees, the sky, the sea, the wind, everything went almost unseen. Then something began to happen. It really began with a creature found by the riverside. First the creature was thought to be a creature from the water which had found itself on land. Later, it was suggested that the creature had dropped down from the sky. "And if," one of Earth's creatures, who called himself man, said at once, "if this creature dropped from the sky, it cannot be a creature, at all, but one of God Almighty's messengers."

"But even," another man-species decided, "but even if it did come from the water, it must also be the Almighty's messenger, for water creatures as a rule cannot live on land."

Fear filled the man-species. They had never wanted to tamper with God's messenger but felt sure they could not just leave it lying there. So, man carefully picked up the creature which was so tiny, so gentle, so soft that man decided to let the most gentle of their species look after this messenger of God. The most gentle of man-species selected one particular woman who was to wash and feed the messenger while others looked on. This special woman fed the messenger from her breast, keeping it from rain and sun, from wind and everything that could harm it.

Gradually, the messenger began to grow bigger. He began to hop about with the others.

One day, the man-species, who had been feeding the messenger from her breast, decided that this messenger should have a name. He should be called something which would distinguish him as different from and special to all other of Earth's creatures. A meeting was called. Everyone came. Man and beast, nearby trees, all listened attentively.

"We shall call him Gado-pikin," said the man-species who had been feeding the messenger from her breast.

All the creatures at the meeting agreed. The trees bowed and nodded their heads in agreement. The birds chirped or howled depending on their voices. The nearby river roared its agreement, while the sky just smiled happily. The Goddess of lightning, thunder and rain, and all who had been looking on and listening, smiled and agreed that this creature was to be Gado-pikin. He was truly God Almighty's own child; so the name of "God's child" was most suitable.

As moon and sun went past, the Gado-pikin grew stronger and bigger. He spent a great deal of his time by the riverside and at times did not speak at all.

"He wants something," Earth's creatures decided. So Earth's creatures brought him food of the best kind, drink of the very best. The creatures were afraid of breaking into the Gado-pikin's silence and therefore had no choice but to leave the food and gifts silently by the riverside. Each day, when the creatures returned, they found that some of the food had disappeared, but some, the very best, was placed on a tree trunk, which was beautifully carved all round its body. With the food there were beautiful and scented flowers.

One day, the wisest of the man-species decided that the Gado-pikin would be wanting and pining for a companion. He felt sure that everyone, man and beast, flower and tree, all needed a companion he could call his very own. A meeting was called. Earth's creatures never did anything without first calling a meeting.

"We must send him a companion to live with him by the riverside," said the wisest of the man-species.

"But we don't know what kind he likes," said the second-wisest of the man-species.

"Let's select the best from among our maidens," said the third-wisest of the man-species.

Now, there were many beautiful maidens but each had her own kind of beauty. Therefore, it was difficult to decide; so, what man did was to send a selected group each day and make them parade by the riverside. The maidens all tried to win the Gado-pikin's interest but he would not even so much as look at them.

As the Gado-pikin continued to live that lonely life and reject all the advances of the maidens, the Earth's creatures really began to worry. One day, someone suggested it could be that the Gado-pikin was so good, he did not want to have a beautiful maiden as companion but preferred to give an ugly maiden a chance. So, the man-species went all round the earth to find the ugliest maiden; in those days there were not many ugly maidens around, for any ugly creature born, any deformed creature born, used to have its life taken from it. Finally, the creatures found a maiden who was living in a hiding-place. She had a very big belly; so, the creatures named her Bijibere (Big Belly). The creatures dragged out the ugly maiden and forced her to go by the riverside and laugh for the Gado-pikin. The maiden had no choice; she had to do what the man-species who were more beautiful than she told her to do. As soon as the maiden got to the riverside and saw the Gado-pikin she began to laugh. She laughed and laughed, and continued laughing for several moons and suns, but no amount of laughter brought even a glance from the Gado-pikin, who just threw pieces of

46

earth into the river. Suddenly, the maiden began to laugh sincerely, for she thought it really funny that a man-species so handsome, with such a beautiful body, with such a shining face and skin, would want her as a companion. The maiden laughed and laughed. She could not stop laughing. She laughed until suddenly her big belly burst with a loud bang.

Many moons and many suns passed before the Earth's man-species found another maiden living in a hiding-place. This maiden had a very big head so she was named Biji-ede (Big Head). The creatures dragged the maiden to the river-side and forced her to sit by the Gado-pikin and nod her head to whatever he may say.

Biji-ede had no choice but to do whatever the man-species who were more beautiful than she told her to do. The maiden sat for many moons and suns but the Gado-pikin said nothing; he just threw pieces of earth into the river. Finally, an idea came to the maiden. "Why not nod my head whether he says something or not?" She nodded her head. Once, twice, three times. Suddenly, she saw the Gado-pikin looking up at her. She saw a smile gradually begin to form on the Gado-pikin's face.

The small smile from the Gado-pikin was very en-couraging; so, the maiden nodded her head, again and again. The more she nodded the broader the smile of the Gado-pikin. The broader the smile of the Gado-pikin the more the maiden shook and nodded. Faster and faster she nodded until the Gado-pikin began to laugh heartily, for he felt the maiden looked funny nodding her head like that. The maiden, however, took the Gado-pikin's laughter for something else and she was sure that he was sooner or later going to want her, an ugly maiden, as his companion; faster and harder the maiden nodded her head. For several moons and suns, without stopping, the maiden nodded her head until suddenly, pop! with a big crack the maiden's big head fell off.

47

Many a moon and sun went by before man-species decided that they must send someone else, but this time they were to do things in a different way. A meeting was called and it was decided that for the last time an ugly maiden was to be chosen. The man-species had great faith in the plan they had in mind. The birds, the trees, the flowers, the sea, all had great faith in the plan the man-species had in mind.

This time, the maiden they found had very skinny legs; so, she was named Fini-voetoe (Thin Leg). After carefully listening to instructions, Fini-voetoe set out for the riverside. She was scared because she had heard that the two ugly maidens who went before her had not returned. However, Fini-voetoe had no choice but to do whatever the man-species more beautiful than she told her to do. When Fini-voetoe came to the riverside, however, and saw the bodies of the two ugly maidens by the feet of Gado-pikin, she got very scared, indeed. Without much fuss, she ran away from the riverside. She ran very fast, forgetting all about her skinny legs. She ran for many moons and many suns, then suddenly, pap! with one big screech like that of a fallen tree, the thin legs of Fini-voetoe snapped.

Sadly, man-species realized that it was no use trying to force a companion on the Gado-pikin. They, however, felt that something had to be done to cheer the Gado-pikin; so, another meeting was held. No one at the meeting had any idea what to do next. The wind said he had no idea. The sky said, "Don't ask me; I am too far away." The trees danced from side to side, waved their branches rhythmically, but came up with no answer to the problem. It was the man-species who had fed the Gado-pikin from her breast who came up with an answer.

"Let me talk to him," suggested the man-species who had fed the Gado-pikin from her breast.

"You?" asked the wisest among the man-species. "What

can you do? You are gentle and good, I agree, but what can you do?"

"What can you do that we have not done?" asked the second-wisest man.

"What can you do that we cannot do?" asked the third-wisest man, a little angry.

"Let her try!" It was the wind, the wind who was wiser than man, wiser than the moon, wiser than the sun, who spoke at last.

The man-species who had fed the Gado-pikin from her breast went to the riverside. As soon as she and the Gado-pikin set eyes on each other, they both ran forward and hugged each other tightly. They later stopped hugging and sat down to talk for a long time. No one knew what they were talking about, for the two, strangely enough, spoke without opening their mouths. They spoke without a sound coming from either of them. After many moons and many suns, the Gado-pikin and the man-species who had fed the Gado-pikin from her breast hugged, once more, then parted.

"What did he say?" Everyone rushed to meet the man-species who had fed the Gado-pikin from her breast.

"He gave me a reason for his sadness," said the man-species who had fed the Gado-pikin from her breast.

"What is it?" everyone asked.

"What is it? asked the birds and the trees, the sky and the sea. They asked because they were all friends and wanted the Gado-pikin of the man-species to be happy.

"He is sad," began the man-species who had fed the Gado-pikin from her breast, when the meeting was seated. "He is sad, because we never bother to give thanks to our Creator. We never bother to give praise for all of this." The man-species who had fed the Gado-pikin from her breast waved her hand about and pointed to all the beautiful things of the earth. "We eat," continued the man-species who had fed the Gado-pikin from her breast, "we eat, drink, dance, but never give thanks."

"That's so," said the wisest of the man-species.

"That's true, but it need not remain true," said the second-wisest of the man-species.

"That's true, but we can start right now to make amends," said the third-wisest of the man-species.

The Earth's creatures started at once. They selected the best of their food. The best of their drink. They slaughtered the best of their animals. Gathered the best of their flowers. They found a group of maidens, some very beautiful, indeed. The maidens carried the food and drink, the slaughtered animals and flowers, on their heads. The maidens were accompanied by chanters and drummers as they walked along in single file towards the river. By the riverside, they found the Gado-pikin had gone but he had built a beautiful table out of tree trunks. He had carved the side of the tree trunks. He had, however, left no indication as to what should be done with the offering. The Earth's creatures had no choice therefore but to lay the offerings on the tree trunks by the riverside and return to their own living places.

After the creatures returned to their own places, there was much chanting and dancing in praise of their Creator, in praise of all the beautiful things of the earth. While the dancing and chanting went on, the man-species, who had fed the Gado-pikin from her breast, went to find the Gado-pikin. She found him sitting where he always sat, by the riverside. This time, when the two set eyes on each other, there was no hugging. Instead, they at once sat and talked. Later, when some of the man-species came to find the man-species who had fed the Gado-pikin from her breast, they discovered that something had happened to her. She said, "You can't see him now. You can't hear him. Only I can see and hear him." With shining and proud eyes, the man-species, who had fed the

Gado-pikin from her breast, went away with her fellow creatures. Only when she got back to the feasting did she say, "You will have to make one promise. You will have to promise to have one set day when you give thanks and praise to your Creator, give thanks and praise for all the beautiful things of earth you are enjoying."

"Did he, Gado-pikin, say that?"

"Yes, he did."

"Well, we promise!" they chanted a chorus.

The creatures have kept their promise until this day. Until this day, they can be seen in procession going towards the river. The maidens carry the food and drink; the maidens carry the flowers and slaughtered animals. The chanters and drummers follow. Never is the Gado-pikin seen but the creatures know he is there, because he is everlasting.

Occasionally, a good and gentle man-species, who has fed a foundling from her breast, is found. She is then made to take and carry messages to the Gado-pikin. If the Gado-pikin sees fit to give this man-species, who has fed a foundling from her breast, the privilege to see him and speak to him, the Gado-pikin gives that privilege. If the Gado-pikin does not see fit to grant this privilege, he does not do so, and man-species can only go home and hope that next time they will have better luck.

AFTER ONE LIFE
Petronella Breinburg

(Surinam)

Djuka Folk Tale

For a long, a very long time, Death used to leave nothing
but sadness behind his rampage of the world. The sadness was because Death seldom gave full warning. Even
with the warnings of the candle-flies, there was still sadness because Earth's creatures seldom knew who Death's
next victim would be. Even when they did know, the
earth's creatures were always powerless against Death
and his tribes of merciless destroyers.

One of the creatures, who was one day left with such
sadness in her heart, was a very young, very humble, very
gentle creature. She was often thought of as a little
Goddess herself, though not a Gado-pikin because everyone knew how she came to the earth. This young, gentle
and humble creature often sat by the river where everyone was sure she communicated with the great Creator.
Often, other creatures would ask her what the Creator
had said, what the Creator was doing: was the Creator
enjoying the offerings put by the river for him? This
young, gentle and humble creature would often pass on
messages to others. The messages warned of bad things
that would happen to the creatures behaving badly, but
promised a good life and good things for the good
creatures.

One day, the person, whom this very young, very gentle
and very humble creature loved best, was destroyed by
Death's sharp blow. It was a sad story. This very young,
very gentle and very humble creature flung herself onto
the riverbank and cried to the great Creator, "If I must
lose my loved one, let me, at least, know what will happen

to my loved one, the one who fed me gentle food from her breast, protected me, caressed me; let me know what will happen to her."

While the very young, very gentle and very humble creature cried up to the sky, which really was the abode of the great Creator but the creatures did not know this, all Earth's creatures looked on, waiting, hoping the Almighty would answer.

The Almighty did answer but only this very young, very gentle and very humble creature heard it. When the others asked her what was said, she was a little reluctant to say, for she feared that the others would not believe her. But the others insisted and promised to believe her whatever she said.

"Well," began this very gentle, very young and very humble creature, "Our Creator, the great Almighty, said not to worry. He said that our loved ones live on in another world."

"She's a big liar!" Only one creature was doubtful, but once one creature is doubtful other creatures become doubtful, too.

"She's a big liar, I tell you," the first creature to be doubtful repeated, over and over again, until others joined him.

"Yes, how do we know that is what he said? You can say anything!" Another shouted his doubt.

"No, she is not a liar." One creature got really scared, because Earth's creatures in those days did terrible things to liars. "She imagines it in her grief. She thinks that is what he said. Not so, very gentle one?"

"No, that is what he said." This very young, very gentle and very humble creature stayed by her word. "That is what he said. Our loved ones are happy and still alive."

The creatures did not believe a word this very young,

very gentle and very humble creature said, and threw her in the river. The earth's creatures went about their work, did their dances, their singing, had their feasting. At one of these feasts, which was being carefully watched by the Moon, the earth's creatures saw a strange thing. They saw the very young and very humble and very gentle creature, whom they had thrown in the river, coming towards them; needless to say the creatures ran like the wind, because they were very frightened; no creature who had been thrown in the river ever came out again.

"I haven't come to stay," the very young, very humble creature said in a strange voice. "I only want to say I have seen the place. I have seen other things as well. You, you who are bad, so bad you throw creatures meant to live on land into the river, you who beat and rob others, have very hard work ahead."

The creatures did not dare speak, they were so frightened. They did not know really what they were frightened about, yet they shivered in fright and apprehension in a corner, and hugged one another to stop each other from shivering their lives out.

"You will work until your bones crack and blood oozes out your bodies," this very young and very humble creature continued. "You see them candles up in the sky?" She pointed up above, and waited to see if the creatures were looking in the direction she was pointing.

The creatures all looked in the direction this very, very young, very gentle and very humble creature, who had returned from the belly of the river into which she was thrown, was pointing; they would not have dared not look there.

"You see them candles? You shall be made to hold them up until the sun comes up. You shall hold them up to show the way to good creatures, to show the way to Moon and all his friends. You shall hold them up and if any one of you should let one fall, you shall wander on

earth until you find that candle. That any one of you who lets that candle fall shall never find peace until that candle is found and replaced in its place in the sky. If that candle is never found, that one of you who lets it fall shall never rest." This humble creature, who had returned from the river into which she was thrown, suddenly took the shape of a big bulky cloud and went back into the sky.

Long after the very young, very humble creature had disappeared into the sky, the earth's creatures, who were feasting, remained close together. For a long time no one dared breathe. Then suddenly someone remembered that they had not offered the very young creature, who had returned from the river into which she was thrown, any food or drink.

"Maybe she'll come back some other time," one of the creatures suggested, but at the same time did not want the very young, very humble creature, whom they had thrown into the river, to return; there was something frightening about that creature.

"No, she'll not come back," said someone else; actually, what that person meant was that he would be afraid to see that creature, whom they had thrown into the river, return. "But, but, we can leave her some food in case she comes. Just in case, mind you."

Every creature agreed that they should have left some food and drink by the entrance where the feasting was going on. They thought that if the food was by the entrance, the creature, who had returned from the river into which they had thrown her, would not bother to enter the feasting inside. They also thought they had better prepare something special, something sacred, because that creature, who had returned from the river into which they had thrown her, must be sacred to be in such close contact with the great Almighty.

So, every creature went out in search of something

special to prepare for the very young and very humble creature. It was another gentle creature who found something special for meat. The something special was an animal which was very clean, because it always hid in its shell. Only the feet and head of the small animal ever touched anything unclean. Anyhow, the head and feet need not be used for this very humble creature who had returned from the river into which they had thrown her.

Every creature set to work. The carvers among them quickly made a small tree-trunk into a place on which to offer that special food and drink to that creature who had returned from the river into which they had thrown her. The gentler creatures among them slaughtered the special animal, making sure that the head and feet, which often came out of its shell, did not touch the sacred part of the body. These gentler creatures prepared other special food and drink from their best trees.

Everything was ready, so every creature gathered at the place of feasting. After gathering, they thought they had better sing a little, in order to please the creature who had returned from the belly of the river into which they had thrown her. So, they sang, and in singing, they told the creature that they had slaughtered and prepared for her a very young and very gentle and very humble animal. They had named the very young, very gentle and very humble animal they had prepared for her, a Sikri-patoe. They had prepared for her roasted corn from the best fields, had prepared for her drink from the best fruits. They had prepared for her enough food, so that she may bring some of the other loved ones who had gone before her to that other place. They wished her to be happy and wished her to speak to the great Almighty on their behalf.

For a long time the creatures sang, but paused now and again to rest. They counted that they had sung for seven moons and seven suns before the food and drink they left outside had gone. After the food and drink had all gone, the earth's creatures gave praise and thanked the sacred one, who had returned from the river into which they had thrown her, to feast on the food and drink left for her. They thanked her and made a promise. They made and have kept their promise until this day because whenever Death rampaged over the earth, taking away one's loved or unloved ones — but mostly loved ones — the creatures would have a feast. They would slaughter that very young, very humble animal which they had named Sikri-patoe, and offer it to the departed one. They would sing and feast for seven days until all the food had been offered and all the drink taken. After the food had gone, they would lift their eyes to the sky and smile happily, knowing that the good creatures had gone behind those lighted candles. They would then ask that creature, who had returned from the river into which they had thrown her, to ask the Almighty for mercy for those holding and keeping those candles in the sky alight. When a candle fell, the creatures would say a silent prayer, so that the one who let it fall would find it soon, so that he may find peace.

Because the candles fallen are seldom found, the creatures, who let them fall, wander around. When they get tired, they become very angry and evil. They destroy man and beast, flowers and trees, without mercy. They often become tools for Death and help Death in his rampages over the earth. Those creatures, who have let the candles fall, often make other creatures evil, so that they can get help and rebel against the great Almighty who made them hold the candles in the first place. The creatures, who have let the candles fall, more often than not, succeed in finding followers, but never are they able to overpower the great Almighty, and will have to go on holding and go on searching for fallen candles for ever.

BRE'R TOUCOOMA IN TROUBLE
Knolly La Fortune
(Trinidad and Tobago)   Folk Tale

Compere Tigg's garden had a good year. Indeed, so many pumpkins were produced that every neighbour in the village shared in his success.

One pumpkin grew so large that he had to ask Bre'r Toucooma to help him take it home. Bre'r Toucooma was not so fortunate, although he had boasted that he would produce the best and biggest pumpkin of the year.

Bre'r Toucooma, therefore, decided on a plan. He would have a great feast. He would invite Crab, Bre'r Agouti, Bre'r Anansi, and Congorie. Together they would devise a scheme to put a "spell" on Compere Tigg's pumpkin field. Fewer pumpkins would grow. Tigg's field would be ruined.

Bre'r Toucooma sent out invitations to some of his closest friends. They would be private invitations. Each letter would be wrapped in banana leaves and tied with strong lianas. Each letter would also have the imprint of Bre'r Toucooma's forefinger at the top right hand corner. These prints were to be indelible. The ink would be made from the seeds of the Black Shade trees. The colour would be deep blue.

Bre'r Anansi promised to take the invitations to each guest. But he was advised by Bre'r Toucooma to carry the invitations at night. Bre'r Anansi usually slept best at night. Most of his activities in Manzanilla Forest took place during the day. Daylight enabled him to work well and to prepare for the rainy season.

On this occasion, Bre'r Anansi was determined to help Bre'r Toucooma, even if it cost him his life. He could not forget how history had taught him that it was Bre'r Toucooma who had saved the Anansi family during the great Brigand Hill forest fires, ages ago.

But tragedy was to befall Bre'r Anansi. Bre'r Agouti was to be given a special invitation, which contained important information about Bre'r Toucooma's plans.

Bre'r Anansi set out at 8 o'clock to find Agouti's home. When he got to the top of Boodoo Hill, he saw a bright light far in the distance. This light he thought should take him to Agouti's den which was deep into the forest. He began to shout:

"Bre'r Agouti, Oh!
Bre'r Agouti, Oh!
Compere Anansi coming!
Compere Anansi coming, Oh!"

There was no reply, except the sound of his own voice which returned to him clear and loud. Bre'r Anansi continued to walk towards the light. As he got nearer and nearer, the whole forest seemed ablaze by a huge blue flame. The flame spun round and round. Then Bre'r Anansi heard sweet sounds. Here and there lights flickered from the heads of moving objects.

Bre'r Anansi approached quietly. Sometimes he hid behind trees and low bushes. Suddenly, a blinding light flashed into his eyes. He was seized by its brilliance. At the same time a voice said:

"Come, join our dance, my friend!
Come, join our dance!
You are welcome!
You are welcome!"

The voice was that of Candle-fly. Candle-fly greeted Bre'r Anansi with dignity. He had three attendants. Each attendant carried a lighted torch.

Three more attendants followed. They were all beautifully dressed. In their outstretched arms they carried Calabashes filled with palm wine.

"Drink our wine,
My friend!
Drink our wine!"

Candle-fly was laughing gleefully. Bre'r Anansi, for the first time, felt hypnotised. He placed the wine to his lips and drank. At first slowly, then quickly. Bre'r Anansi began to feel sweet rhythmic sensations run through his veins. Warm beads of perspiration fell from his brow. His head spun. His arms and feet began to move. Bre'r Anansi was dancing, dancing, and humming a merry tune:

"Te, Te, Tum, Te, Tum,
Te, Te, Tum, Te, Tum,
Tra, la, la, la, la,
Tee, Tum . . ."

By this time, Bre'r Anansi was surrounded by a host of Candle-flies. They were of all shapes and sizes. Some were singing strange tunes. Some were dancing on one leg. While some flitted through the leaves.

After four hours of feasting, Bre'r Anansi fell to the ground. He was soon fast asleep. While he slept, Candle-fly searched him thoroughly. The personal letter addressed to Bre'r Agouti was found. The address read:

"Bre'r Augustus Archibald Agouti, Esq.,
Bois-Ban-dey Reserve,
Manzanilla North,
Forest Region,
Manzanilla, No. 4.

When the letter was read, Bre'r Toucooma's mischievous plot was discovered. The party was stopped immediately. Candle-fly decided to take the letter to Compere Tigg. He travelled the rest of the night and arrived at 5 o'clock in the morning.

Compere Tigg was awakened by sweet melodious voices. There were friends who would like to speak to him. He opened his bedroom window, yawned, and said:

"Welcome, my friends,
What news, at this time of a morning?
What news? What news?"

Candle-fly cleared his throat and said, "Peace, peace be with you, Compere Tigg. There is evil in the air."

Candle-fly and his followers were asked to enter. They were given bowls filled with wild honey to refresh themselves. The points in the letter were then discussed. It was decided to call a general meeting of all the forest animals. Bre'r Toucooma was summoned at once. He would be made to answer charges of conspiring with Bre'r Anansi to destroy Compere Tigg's good reputation as the finest pumpkin producer in the land.

When Bre'r Toucooma heard the news, he became frightened. He knew that there was one punishment for this crime. Forest laws laid down death by drowning in Grand Lagoon. Then burial in Crows Cemetery. By this time Bre'r Anansi had already disappeared. So Toucooma decided to run for his life. But before he could make his escape, Compere Tigg, Centipede, Scorpion, Mappire-Zanana, and T-Macajuel were hot on his trail.

"My problem", Toucooma said to himself, "is where to hide. Hog-plum tree must be avoided at all costs. Bois-canoe is too exposed to the wind; the scent of my body would spread like wildfire. Damit!" Stamping his feet, he said, "Is Gru-gru-bef for me, we."

So Bre'r Toucooma made up his mind to hide at the very top of a Gru-gru-bef tree. Now, Gru-gru-bef is one of the most prickly palms in North Manzanilla Forest.

All Gru-gru-bef trees were manned by Scorpions, and by Centipedes. Besides that, below them lay Mappire-Zanana and T-Macajuel. They were all waiting for Toucooma to fall. Even Metivere-grass and Mazia-Marie set their ears for any suspicious sounds or movements.

So crick, crack,
Monkey break he back
In ah crab trap!

THE CHILDREN'S FRIEND
Vishnu R. Gosine
(Trinidad and Tobago)   Folk Tale

Few people in Ouplay claimed they were friends of Ma
Coo-coo. This was not because they quarrelled frequently
with her, or refused to have anything to do with the old
woman. No. It was not that. Ma Coo-coo was not sociable.
She seldom spoke, and when she did, her words were few.

For Ma Coo-coo, Ouplay offered the peace and quietness that no other village offered. It was situated about
one mile off the main road, and few vehicles passed in
front of her house. This quietness meant much. She
wanted to be alone, and free from the interference of
anyone or anything.

For the two years she lived in Ouplay, the villagers paid
her no special attention. But recently their curiosity was
aroused. A story had originated, nobody knew exactly
where, that Ma Coo-coo was a *soucouyant*! Once she
sucked a woman and nearly drained all the blood from
her body. The woman fell critically ill, and had it not
been for a swift blood transfusion, she would have died
and left her five children homeless.

Another person claimed that from the news she received
from her sister, who lived in St. Andrew's Village, Ma
Coo-coo loved children's blood. And to ensure that her
victims did not wake up while she sucked them, she would
cast a spell which would put them into a deep sleep.
Twice she sucked children who immediately became weak
from the excessive loss of blood, and for a few weeks they
were listless and drowsy.

The villagers kept a close watch on their children,
sternly warning them not to accept sweets from Ma Coo-

64

coo. This was not their only way of fighting her. They kept a constant, nightly vigil over her house, hoping that she would leave one night and they would catch her.

After three nights of constant watch over her house, they lost their enthusiasm. They thought that the stories they heard of Ma Coo-coo had come from a group, who was bent on making mischief. But Bobo, who knew a little about witchcraft, did not dismiss the rumour.

He told his neighbour, "Take what I tell you. It have some truth in that. Everything you hear have some truth in it."

One night Bobo was returning from a late cinema show. He was feeling tired and sleepy, and yawned every two minutes. He had just entered Railway Road which led to Ouplay Village, when he saw a small, dim light rising slowly above the village. Bobo's sleepiness deserted him instantly. He wanted evidence and now he had found it. But he could not definitely say it was Ma Coo-coo who flew away, since he was so far from the place. But the best way to ascertain that Ma Coo-coo was or was not the *soucouyant* was to visit her home. If he found her at home, he would know she was not the *soucouyant*; but if he found the house empty, it meant she was the *soucouyant*!

Bobo crept silently near her window. He peeped inside and saw Ma Coo-coo sleeping cosily under a white sheet. Her face was hidden but a little of her forehead was visible. Bobo was satisfied that she was at home. Now that he knew that Ma Coo-coo was at home, it meant that someone else in Ouplay was practising this form of witchcraft.

Two nights later, he saw the same light rising slowly above the village. He again visited Ma Coo-coo and again discovered that she was at home. She was on her bed sleeping in the same position and covered with the same sheet. This made Bobo very suspicious. He was determined to find out who the *soucouyant* was, and so he called Ma Coo-coo who did not even stir at all.

Bobo threw a few stones in her house, but even the noise of the crashing stones failed to wake her. So Bobo, left without an alternative, unlatched a window and entered. He called again but still there was no response. "But is funny, yes! This 'oman like she dead or what?" Bobo pulled the white sheet from above her and what he saw confirmed his belief. Ma Coo-coo was not under the sheet! A dummy, stuffed in cloth, was in her place.

"Well, I tell you, this 'oman really smart," he told him-

self. "So, this is the secret, eh? Well, I go show you." He bit his cracked up lips and ground his teeth. "I will make you shame, 'oman." He pointed to the dummy. "I will teach you a lesson you will never forget."

Without losing any time, Bobo hurried to inform the people of his discovery. He wanted them to know that there was truth in the rumours they heard, and that they must now join forces and catch Ma Coo-coo.

About eight men gathered around Ma Coo-coo's house, and decided to wait. Some went inside and poured salt on her skin. They felt confident now that Ma Coo-coo could not escape. She must return before the break of dawn or she would suffer without her skin and so die.

But from experience Ma Coo-coo knew she must return early before the villagers left for work. So at about three o'clock in the morning, after she had sucked enough blood, she decided to return. And on this night she felt the happiest. When Ma Coo-coo talked to children, it was merely to discover who were healthy and unhealthy. On this night her victims were two children, and this pleased her immensely. She felt that children's blood was fresh, and healthier than the blood of elders.

Ma Coo-coo's landing on the ground was as noiseless as the hopping of a bird. Her walk was slow, and Bobo attributed this to her overfilled stomach of human blood. The men who were hiding in the house did not emerge immediately. When Ma Coo-coo entered the house, she was satisfied that no one had interefered with her dummy, and that everything was in the same position as she had left it.

Under her bed she found her skin and quickly jumped into it! Immediately she cried in pain! The salt which Bobo and his men had rubbed lightly on it had taken effect. It had touched her naked flesh! Her cries were loud and wild as though someone was beating her. Ma Coo-coo quickly threw off the skin.

The men who were hiding in the house now revealed themselves. When Ma Coo-coo saw them surround her, she knew she could no longer deny she was *soucouyant*. She begged the men to forgive her, but they were bent on punishing her further. Kanhai pulled out a cross from his pocket, and pushed it in front of Ma Coo-coo's face. But she ducked and hid from it. She cried out saying that she was feeling painful vibrations inside her; she shouted and screamed and begged the men to forgive her, and spare her this torture, but they did not stop. They continued to torture her with the cross.

Despite her cries for mercy, the villagers decided they could not set her free. But since she had sucked no one

from Ouplay, they would merely banish her from the village, and she must promise never to suck anyone again. And if she broke this promise, the penalty would be death!

Ma Coo-coo promised faithfully to obey Bobo's commands.

The next day nobody saw Ma Coo-coo. In the afternoon, two men were seen breaking down her house. Later that evening a truck transported the materials away.

The only ones who missed Ma Coo-coo were the children, and they soon forgot her. But the elders remembered her story, and whenever their children were troublesome, their mothers would threaten them, "You better sleep fast, yes, or else Ma Coo-coo go suck you tonight." The children would grow afraid, and in a few minutes' time would fall asleep. The parents would be happy, for they could now continue their "ole talk" or household chores without interruption.

THE TALKING DONKEY
Vishnu R. Gosine
(Trinidad and Tobago)   Folk Tale

Not too long ago, Jai reflected that he used to squat on
the pavement with the other boys. Sometimes they sat
outside the rumshops on tall, wooden stools, and lingered
and whistled girls who passed on the roads. Or they would
spread empty sugar sacks on the ground, and spend the
afternoon drinking Vat 19. And to entertain themselves
further, they would beat empty bottles and tins they found
around.

Today, seven years later, he secretly congratulated his
father for dragging him out of that circle of friends, who
saw the world as only a place to drink rum and make
merry. His father wanted progress, and to him progress
did not mean buying more rum, or spending more time
lingering on the pavement; it meant acquiring more
fertile lands on which to grow more food crops.

Jai's father saw as far as that point, but after a few
years of hard labour, Jai saw further. He was a young
man and did not want to work forever as a labourer. He
wanted to be a powerful land owner and agriculturist, and
have people work for him. This he achieved by hard work
and determination. He was happy. His wife and children
were also happy. But his friends, with whom he once
squatted, were sad. Some farmers, however, felt his progress had been too rapid.

One morning, Jai visited his garden, and discovered
that holes had been cut in the mounds of his ricelands,
and that the water had leaked away; the *bodi* and lettuce
picked, and some destroyed and thrown on the ground.
Jai calculated the cutting of the mounds was surely done

by man, but he could not think that someone sane would utterly destroy the fruits he didn't want! It had to be the work of a vandal, he thought. On closer inspection, Jai saw large hoof marks on the ground, and there and then was sure that an animal had destroyed his vegetables. But whose animal? he asked himself.

Jai dismissed the thought from his mind. Perhaps it was just a stubborn donkey that had been let loose, he concluded. But he was puzzled about the cutting of the holes. He could not understand how an animal could cut holes! Two nights later, another such raid was made on his garden, and more crops destroyed. This time, he boiled in anger. It was a deliberate act to destroy his crops, he summed up.

Jai visited Pundit Sharma and related his misfortune. The Pundit consulted his astrological book and told him that someone in the village was jealous of him.

"Jealous of me? Why for they jealous? I work hard. I stop liming. That doesn't pay."

"This is how people is," the Pundit said.

"You think you could tell me who the person is?" Jai asked.

The Pundit again consulted his book. He muttered something and then shook his head. "Is not that easy. The most I seeing here is something like a donkey, but...."

"That self!" Jai interrupted. "Is a donkey."

"So you know?" Pundit Sharma asked him. "But be careful. Is a strange kind of donkey."

Later that evening at about seven o'clock, Ramnath, one of Jai's employees, told him of a strange thing he observed: "It go sound strange to you but is something I really see. I was passing by Lal Beharry Trace just now, and I see a donkey tie to tree. Is a strange kind of donkey. It was big and brown and it had a cutlass tie to it belly."

71

"A what? A cutlass?" Jai asked almost disbelieving his ears.

"Yes, but that is not all. The donkey look at me and give me a wink eye. And then it bend down again and start to eat grass again. As I walk off, I hear a voice say, 'Tonight! Tonight!' I look around but I didn't see anybody. So I continue to walk. When I reach Harriman Trace, I see a next donkey. I look at it good and see it is the same donkey. And it giving me a kind of cross-eye look. It say again, 'Tonight! Tonight!' "

"It had anything tie around it neck?" Jai asked impatiently.

"A chain. A thin one."

"Blasted *lagahoo*. I go do for that bitch."

Jai was going to pursue this *lagahoo* with a purpose. He

72

felt that because the animal talked and wore a chain around its neck, it was a *lagahoo.* And since a cutlass was strapped around it, this further confirmed his belief. Jai thought that just before the person changed into a *lagahoo,* he strapped this cutlass around his naked body, and perhaps this was the same instrument with which he dug holes into the mounds and allowed the water to escape.

To reach his garden, Jai and Ramnath did not travel on the road used by most people. Instead they used a road which brought them at the back of the garden. The two walked briskly, without saying anything. Jai was very concerned as to who in the village would wish to destroy his crops. Well, tonight he was going to stop the enemy once and for all. He was going to chop the animal so that when it returned to its human form, the cut would be seen by all.

When they reached the garden, they heard sounds of scratching, nipping, and of someone rushing savagely, almost desperately, to attack something. Then it seemed things were dragged away, and this was followed by the stamping of feet. At this time, heavy chains clanged, and Ramnath and Jai felt confident that the donkey was in the garden. It was the right moment to attack and punish the *lagahoo.*

On the way to the garden, Jai had cut a piece of wood from a nearby gauva tree. This he gave to Ramnath. The two decided that if they could not destroy the *lagahoo.* they should at least give him a mark he would always remember.

Ramnath saw the donkey destroying some plants. He emerged from behind a few corn plants and charged at the animal, holding the club-like wood in his hand, ready to crash it on the donkey's head. The donkey, as though it had been warned, raised its head, saw Ramnath, and side-stepped him. Ramnath missed his target and fell.

73

Without trying to attack the fallen Ramnath, the talking donkey shouted, "Bitch!" and dashed to escape.

It had almost run past Jai when his cutlass flashed in the darkness and descended on him. A loud cry of a man in pain was heard. Then further shouts of "Is me! Is me!" were heard.

Ramnath was still lying on the ground when Jai hurried to his side. "Anything wrong?" Jai asked.

"No. Not really. You chop him?" Ramnath asked.

"I sure is one foot he will have," Jai said. "Is a good blow."

That night the whole of Ouplay was told the story. Then everyone became curious to know who the *lagahoo* might be. It was not long after, Ramlal, who pretended to be a *sadhu*, was found bleeding from a severe chop on his left leg. He was ashamed and asked the few villagers who discovered this, not to communicate the news to the others.

But the news could not be withheld, and soon the whole village knew that Ramlal was a *lagahoo*. Whenever children saw him in the streets, they always shouted, "Lagahoo Ramlal!" He would then curse them, and try to hit them with his walking stick. But he could never catch them; he was too slow.

ANANCY AND SORREL
Louise Bennett
(Jamaica)   Anancy Folk Tale

Once upon a Christmas Eve morning, it was Grand
Market morning and Bredda Anancy stood by his gate-
way watching all the people going down to the market.
The baskets on their heads and the hampers on the
donkeys were laden with fruits and flowers and ground
provisions. Anancy called out, "Happy Grand Market,
everybody!"

"Thank you, Bredda Anancy!" replied the people.

Anancy said to himself, "Wat a crosses pon me! It look
like say everybody pick off everything offa every tree an
carry gawn a Grand Market."

Anancy groaned as a cart-load of oranges and grape-
fruits went by. "Massi me Massa, dem don't leave a ting
eena de field dem fe me to scuffle."

Anancy waited until everybody had passed on their
way to the market and then he went from field to field
in search of scufflings.

"Wat a hard set of people, sah!" Anancy grieved.
"Dem clean out everything outa de field dem. Not a
chenks a scuffling fe me."

Suddenly, Anancy exclaimed, 'Wat a sinting so red!'
And he broke a long stalk of a long red plant and held it
to his nose.

"It don't got no sweet smell," said Anancy, "but it
pretty fe look pon. I wonder wat it good for?"

Anancy picked a few more stalks of the red plant and
stuck them in his trousers waist, mumbling to himself,
"Well, den, since you is the only ting I can scuffle, I scuffling you, Red Sinting. I don't know wat I going to do wid
you yet. I don't know if you can eat, but I might even
haffe eat you."

Anancy laughed, "Kya, kya, kya, kya!"

He danced and sang, all the way to the Grand Market. When he got there, Anancy looked around at all the beautiful stalls, full of fruit-kind and food-kind and cooked food and food cooking. Anancy said to himself, "I will have to work up me brains and find a way to raise something."

He stopped in front of a stall with plenty otaheiti apples, pointed to the red plant in his trousers waist and said to the stall-keeper, "Hi, Missis, swap me some a fe you red tings fe some a fe me red tings."

The woman asked him, "Wat fe you red tings name?"

Anancy said, "Swap me, first."

The woman said, "Tell me, first."

Anancy said, "Swap me, first."

The woman replied, "Tell me, first, an I will swap you."

A woman in a pumpkin stall next to the woman's otaheiti stall shouted, "Missis, if you want de red ting, why you don't just grab it away from de little man!"

Anancy laughed, "Kya, kya, kya, kya!" and shouted back, "Grab it if you bad!"

A man grabbed after Anancy. Anancy said, "Slip!" and ran.

The man chased Anancy through the market. Several people joined in the chase, shouting, "Tief, tief, catch de tief!"

Anancy kept slipping them, darting in and out of the stalls, until he reached a hominy stall.

The hominy-lady had a big jester-pot full of boiling water on the fire. She was just about to drop the hominy corn into the pot, when Anancy flung the bundle of red plant into the boiling water.

The hominy-lady screamed, "Wat dat you throw into me pot?"

The crowd rushed up to the pot, and one man exclaimed, "It red like blood! It favour wine!"

Anancy looked into the pot and laughed, "Kya, kya, kya, kya!" And then, he shouted, "It don't only look like wine; is wine!"

"Wine! Wine!" the crowd exclaimed. "Make we taste it!"

Anancy mumbled to himself, "Poor me boy, a hope is not poison."

The man who had started the chase rushed forward, grabbed a spoon and tasted the liquid. He made up his face and said, "It don't got no taste."

Anancy said, "It don't finish brew yet.

      It want some sugar,
      A little ginger,
      A piece of cinnamon.
      And then you stir so.
      And then you stir so."

And Anancy took a little of all the spices from the hominy-lady's stall, and threw them into the pot. Anancy tasted the brew. "Kya, kya, kya, kya!" Anancy laughed. "It taste nice, like real-real wine."

The hominy-lady said, "It smell nice!"

Anancy looked fondly into the pot and whispered in wonderment, "How you so real, so real, so real!"

Somebody in the crowd shouted, "It name So-real! Sell me tru-pence wut a So-real!"

The crowd took up in chorus, "Tru-pence Sorreal! Tru-pence Sorreal!"

Anancy brewed and sold So-real, all day. It was the most popular drink at the Grand Market. By the end of the day, in our own true fashion, So-real had become Sorrel. And from that day to today, Sorrel is a famous Christmas drink. Is Anancy make it.

Jack Mandora, me no choose none.

ANANCY AND COMMONSENSE
Louise Bennett

(Jamaica)   Anancy Folk Tale

Once upon a time, Anancy, feeling very greedy for power and wealth, decided to collect all the commonsense there was in the world. He thought that everyone would then have to come to him with their problems and he would charge dear for his advice. So, he set out to collect all the commonsense in the world.

He collected and he collected, and all that he found, he put in a large calabash. When he could find no more commonsense, he sealed the calabash with a roll of dry leaves. Then, he decided to hide all the commonsense, at the top of a very high tree, so that no one else could get at it.

Anancy tied a rope to the neck of the calabash, tied the two ends of the rope together and put the loop over his head, so that the calabash rested on his stomach.

He started to climb the tree, but found that the calabash was getting in his way. He tried again and again, but all in vain. Suddenly, he heard someone laughing behind him, and looked around to see a little boy.

"Stupid fellow," cried the little boy, "if you want to climb the tree, why don't you put the calabash behind you?"

Anancy was so annoyed to hear this little bit of commonsense coming from a little boy, when he, Anancy, thought that he had collected it all, that he flung the calabash at the foot of the tree and broke it.

And so, commonsense was scattered in little pieces, all over the world, and nearly everyone got a bit of it.

Anancy is the cause.

Legends

Children of the Sun presented by Jan Carew
The Coming of Amalivaca presented by Jan Carew
Timu and the Kunaima presented by Aubrey Williams
A Home Beneath the Clouds presented by Roy Heath
The Legend of Guagugiona presented by Christopher
    Laird

CHILDREN OF THE SUN
Jan Carew
(Guyana)   Amerindian Legend

In long time past days, when Sun was young and free and
his furnace-heat was caged deep inside his heart, the
Great Spirit, who was god of earth and sky and sea, gave
him wings. And often, in a playful mood, Sun soared
along the rim of blue horizons or played games with Wind
and the stars, dodging in and out of the rafters that held
up the sky. Sometimes, when Wind passed by with his
eagle and red heron and cockatoo feathers streaming
behind him, Sun singed his feathers and trails of smoke
in Wind's wake gathered into clouds.

Because Sun was young and free and the Great Spirit
had given him wings, his mind often told him to do things
that were unaccountably reckless and wild. He plunged
into rivers, raising clouds of mist and steam; he danced
until his burning feet started forest fires; and by telling
the stars how beautiful they were, he lured them to gaze
at their images in mirrors of still water, then he caught
them in a net and scattered them like fireflies across
forests and savannahs. Sun spent most of his time making
bacchanal and spreading joy, and when weariness caught
up with him, he lay down anywhere that sleep surprised
him.

While Sun made bacchanal and feted and played
games, there was much confusion and suffering in the
Human World. Long spells of darkness filled the skies,
while Sun slept in the daytime. The corn never ripened;
cassava roots rotted in the cold earth; and there were no
singing birds at day-clean, for night and day threw somer-
saults to match Sun's whims. So, the people and their

elders went to the Great Spirit and complained.

"Great Spirit," they said, "since there is no regular coming and going of our nights and days, we are faced with starvation and death. There is darkness at noon, and a noon-day brightness at night, and when the thirsty Sun returns from his carousing, he drinks up all the water in sight. Our wells are dry and where there was once cool running water there's only wrinkled mud and desolation.

The Great Spirit sat on his gigantic royal stool. Its concave seat was cushioned with moss and striped with a host of rainbow orchids. In a voice that sighed like wind in casuarina trees, he promised, "I will talk to Sun."

As soon as the people and their elders had left, the Great Spirit sent Gé, the Condor-bird, to fetch Sun. Gé found Sun sleeping in a cradle of snow, in the Mountains of the Moon, and every breath Sun took melted the snow and sent water cascading down the mountainsides.

"Sun," Gé croaked. His voice was unmelodius, but he had a gentle heart. "Sun," he repeated.

"Leave me alone. Don't you see I'm weary?"

"Sun, I know you've been fatiguing your body all about the place, and left to me, I would let you sleep on, but the Great Spirit sent me to call you. He says you must come at once."

"Ahhhhhh! Mmmmmmm!" Sun groaned, then he rubbed the sleep out of his eyes, stretched, and getting up, rubbed snow brisky all over his body.

"Coming, Sun?" Gé asked, for he was growing impatient.

"Can't you see I'm coming, Condor-bird?" Sun replied, angrily.

They flew in silence to the mountains of Akarai, where the Great Spirit holds court sitting on his royal stool.

"You must mend your ways, Sun!" The voice of the Great Spirit thundered out of the silences surrounding them. "My people and their elders are complaining about the sufferings you're heaping on their backs."

"I'll change my ways, Great Spirit; I swear I'll change," the chastened Sun said.

"Go well, Sun, and never again make mirth with those at your mercy!"

While the Great Spirit drew a curtain of mists around him, Gé led a contrite Sun away from the silent heights of Akarai.

For a long time afterwards, Sun rose at day-clean and set in the gloaming, and at nights he slept in cool secret caverns under the sea. One day, he rose in the east and in the evenings crept into the western sea caves, and the next day he rose in the west and slept in the east, and in this way he had more time to himself at nights.

One afternoon, when red herons, white cranes, gaudy toucans, sleek wild ducks and raucous parrots were flying home to their nests, Sun saw Tihona sleeping on the white sands, where the Potaro River snaked through the valley. Potaro's lisping tongues sang to her, so softly, that Sun could barely catch its muted melodies, and the sight of a dark and beautiful girl lying on the riverbank made Sun's heart jump. Her skin had the velvet sheen of the petals of a black narcissus, the rarest of all mountain flowers, and her limbs, stretched out carelessly on the sand, looked as if they had flowed there from a rill of dark water. Sun spoke to her in a voice he hardly recognized as his own.

"Dark lady of the white sands of Potaro, what is your name?"

"Tihona, Ti-ho-na!" the mischievous parrots called out.

Sun left the familiar trails he had walked so often in the sky, and without knowing what he was doing, stood on the riverbank to gaze at Tihona. But neither the parrots calling out her name with their piercing voices nor Sun's warm breath woke her up. Instead, she sighed, as though sleep had turned her body into a house of dreams. As Sun bent over her, drops of sweat from his brow fell into her black hair, and these became jewels of brightest gold.

"Ti-ho-na! Ti-ho-na!" Parrots, toucans and macaws chorused, and she woke up. She would have fled but Sun reached out and held her. They wrestled on the sand, her fury matching his blind will. But finally, she lay so still, that only the barest heaving of her chest showed that she was still alive. There were jewels of brightest gold in her hair, and others strewn across the sand, like fallen stars, when Sun returned to his station in the sky. Circling the burning horizon, Sun would have kept the doors of heaven locked against the night, forever, if the Great Spirit had not sent Gé to trap him in a net and take him to the caves under the sea.

When morning came, Sun woke up to find himself chained forever to a single trail across the sky, and his wings taken away from him. The Great Spirit had decreed that, as long as the grass grows and as long as the rivers flow, Sun should rise in the East and set in the West, and at nights he had to follow the endless caves under the world to reach his station in the East, at foreday-morning.

Tihona, a warrior Queen, whose father was the keeper of Thunderbolts and whose mother was the lightning Eel, finding herself with child and hating Sun, crossed mountains and valleys, lakes and savannahs, until she came to the seashore. She waited until Sun was setting and called out to him, "Sun, I'll give these twins I'm carrying inside me to the sea."

"I must already pay in suffering for what I've done to you as long as the rivers flow, so spare the twins, Tihona." Sun pleaded, and he fell like a stone beyond the horizon, and stars and fireflies took over the night skies.

Tihona gathered driftwood, and using a speck of fire that Sun had given her, she sat listening to the wet logs hissing like sea serpents; and in the starlight, she could see surf plaiting garlands of foam around dark rocks.

"Mama," a voice called out, startling her, for it was one of the twins.

"Mama," both of them said, "we are your sons, don't give us to the cruel sea."

"I must be carrying devils inside me!" Tihona cried.

"Mama, we are your sons, your own flesh and blood!" The twins chorused.

"Great Spirit, what is this terror nesting in my womb against my will! Help me!" Tihona cried, again.

But the Great Spirit held his tongue and all she could hear was the lisping of the changing tide, the keening wind, and coals bursting in the fire and sending off showers of sparks.

"Mama, we are your sons, the Children of the Sun. Mama, who are you? Your heart beats so fiercely it frightens us. It echoes inside our frail bodies like drums."

She sat down on the sand and sighed. She could feel their tiny fists beating against the walls of her womb.

"I am the daughter of Kabo Tano, Keeper of Thunderbolts, and my mother is the Lightning Eel; everytime she moves there is a flash of lighting," Tihona said.

"Mama . . ." the twins chorused.

"Hush! Go to sleep!" she said gently, and they fell asleep knowing that she had accepted them as her sons.

Tihona lived on the beach, and all the evil reptiles and brute-beasts left her alone. Cormorants brought her fresh fish in the mornings and Gé came daily with supplies of cassava, corn and fruit. The morning after the twins were born, Gé took Tihona and her twins to the top of Roraima, the red mountain, and the Great Spirit named the twins Pia and Makunaima, the Children of the Sun. Hating the twins, at first, Tihona now loved them with a passion bordering on idolatry.

One morning bright with dew and singing birds, Gé came to Tihona and announced, "The Great Spirit says that I must take the Children of the Sun to the Human World."

"Gé, I beg of you, go back and tell the Great Spirit that they're still children. Tell him they're young saplings which any wind can break. In a little while they'll be sturdy enough to stand up to a hurricane. Plead with him for me, Gé!"

"The Great Spirit will not change his mind," Gé said with finality, and Tihona knew that he was telling the truth.

But while Tihona was weaving cloaks out of mists for the twins, Makunaima said, "Mama, let me stay here with you. Pia says it's his duy to go on long journeys. Mama, my dreams are so tormented at nights that if you're not beside me they'll tear me to pieces like fangs and claws. . . . We'll be so happy, you and I, together and all alone, and I'll swear I'll do whatever you say. . ."

He clung to her so fiercely that she cried out, remembering the afternoon, Sun, his father, had wrestled with her on the banks of Potaro. She pushed him away from her and looked at him as though she was seeing him for the first time. Strange fires burned in the depths of his eyes. Pia, bewildered, put his arm around his brother's shoulders and tried to lead him away, but Makunaima struck out at him.

"I'll kill you if you ever touch me again," he said, rushing away until the mountain mists enveloped him.

Fore-day-morning brought pale lightnings, and when day-clean was upon them, they journeyed to the Human World. Gé took them down a forest trail that led to Tihona's house, and went his way. Tihona found her people scattered, and those who remained were sharing their ancestral lands with black strangers, tall ebony men and women with cotton eyes and teeth as white as tiger orchids.

Bewildered, Tihona went to the oracle whose spirit

lived inside a giant silk-cotton tree, and she said, "Oracle of the Lightning Eel, the Tunder Axe, keeper of the secrets of the Great Spirit, is it true what my eyes have seen, that my people are scattered and we share the land with strangers?"

"It's true, Tihona. One morning, huge canoes, parting the waves as easily as sharks, a hundred paddles guiding them, came to our shores and bounding out of them were midnight men with eyes and teeth as bright as stars."

And Makunaima, listening said, "We must drive them out."

But Pia said, "Suppose they came in peace?"

"They came in peace," the Oracle said, "and brought their priests and healers with them, and their magicians can make rain or tame the rainbow."

"And yet, I'm afraid," Tihona said under her breath.

"Go well, Tihona," the Oracle said, retreating into the heart of the giant silk-cotton.

At fore-day-morning, Gé came with messages, once more.

"The Great Spirit says the Children of the Sun must visit him," Gé said.

"But why is he harassing my sons like this, Gé?" Tihona asked.

"Don't ask me; I'm only a messanger," Gé grumbled. "All I know is that the Great Spirit wants to see your sons, lady."

The twins sat on Gé's back, and as he flew over mountains and savannahs, they caught glimpses of people as small as ants below them.

The Great Spirit welcomed the twins, and made them sit beside him on mossy cushions on his great stone stool, Pia on his right and Makunaima on his left.

"Would you like to be good men or great men?" the Great Spirit asked.

And Makunaima answered instantly, "I'd like to be a

89

great man, to have power over men. I'd like to be the keeper of men's fears, to give or take their fears away from them."

And the Great Spirit listening, was silent for a long time before he turned to Pia for his reply.

"I'd like to be a good man," Pia said simply.

"The good must suffer the grief and pains of other men," the Great Spirit said, and Pia felt sorry for him sitting there on his cold stone chair, always alone.

"Why did you send for us, Great Spirit?" Makunaima asked, because the silence was making him uneasy.

"You must go on a journey to the end of the world," the Great Spirit said.

"And who will look after our mother?" Pia asked.

"Why do both of us have to go on this journey, Great Spirit? I can stay at home and look after our mother," Makunaima said.

"You must both go on this journey, and you must set out now," Gé repeated because the Great Spirit had vanished before their eyes.

Through endless seasons they journeyed to the farthest corners of the earth. They sailed down the Rivers of Night with vampires tied to the prows of their canoe, and on a cool and windy evening they came to the Land of Fire. They did everything they could to capture fire and take it back to the world of men, but everytime they tried, the fire died.

One afternoon, they sat beside a mountain pool in the Pakaraimas. On the opposite side of the pool was Wa-uno, the White Crane, who was part magician and part bird. Crane struck his beak against a flint and sent off sparks.

"Do that again, Crane," the twins begged, and Crane struck the flint again and again, and each time sparks flew in all directions.

"We must take this gift of fire to our mama," Makunaima said.

90

"We must take it to all men," Pia said.

"Don't you see, Pia, if we keep this gift of fire for ourselves — you and me and our mama — we'll have more power than the Great Spirit himself!"

"Makunaima, we'll take this gift of fire to all men. Our mama wouldn't want us to steal what belongs to everyone."

And so, the Children of the Sun brought fire to Man. And all who saw fire, for the first time, became its worshippers. It warmed the bones of those who shivered through cold nights and kept the roaming brute-beasts from the haunts of men. There were times when fire showed its power, running before the wind and consuming everything in its path, and leaving in its wake charred and blackened savannahs of desolation.

Wa-uno, the White Crane, then told Pia and Makunaima how difficult it was to fish in rivers which, tumbling down the mountainsides, ran like deer across hills and valleys and plains.

So, the Children of the Sun rewarded Crane for leading them to the gift of fire by rolling gigantic rocks across the rivers, taming the leaping horns of raging water until the streams meandered quietly across the flat and thirsty plains like a shining serpent.

In the daytime, the rivers mirrored the changing moods of the sky, and they were full of stars at night, and the dreaming Moon and maidens vain as parakeets never tired of gazing at their images in the still water.

By taming the rivers, Pia and Makunaima made fishing easier and the people of the Human World rejoiced, because, for the first time, they had become strangers to starvation.

After accomplishing these tasks, Pia and Makunaima returned to their mother. They had left home as boys and were returning as men whose good deeds had made them known in the farthest corners of the earth. They embraced Tihona, and her heart soared like an eagle. She wept, and murmured things that were meaningless, unless you could have seen the changing expressions of fear and joy and relief on her face. The waiting for her sons had streaked her hair with grey and her face, beating against so many anxious years, was indented like a walnut by time and suffering.

At first, Tihona could not really believe that her sons had returned. She woke up in the middle of the night and spent hours gazing at them while they slept. One night, when she was bending over Makunaima, her hair brushed across his eyes, and he woke up. Before she could cry out he lifted her in his arms and ran towards the sacred grove of mora trees that stood like sleepy watchmen around the giant silk-cotton and she could feel his breath like fire and ice on her face. Pia woke up, and seeing a shadowy figure abducting his mother, reached for the only gift that Father Sun had ever given him, a spear made from a shaft of sunlight. He hurled the spear at the retreating figure and it struck home in Makunaima's heart. Makunaima was dead but not a drop of blood stained the innocent grass on which he lay, and snakes formed a circle around his corpse, hissing a devil's requiem all night.

Pia, realising that he had killed his brother, kept a vigil with his mother beyond the circle of snakes and waited for day-clean. As soon as Father Sun appeared, Pia shot arrows in the air, and when they became intertwined with sunlight, he made a ladder out of arrow shafts and sunbeams, said goodbye to his mother and climbed up the ladder until he came to the house of Father Sun. He entered the house and found Father Sun lying in his hammock in an immense circle of light; and Pia noticed that his father had burning anthracite eyes and that his finger and toenails sprouted tongues of flame. Pia greeted his father respectfully. Father Sun welcomed him in turn and offered him a hammock next to his, and when he enquired of Pia why he had come, Pia told him how he had killed his twin brother by accident.

Father Sun, touched by the anguish and despair in his son's voice, said, "Pia, you must return to earth and bring Makunaima's body to my house before I start my journey from the Western caves."

Pia made the journey to and from earth with the speed of a deer, and very gently he placed Makunaima's body in the centre of the largest room in Father Sun's house.

Father Sun melted the spear that had pierced Makunaima's heart and brought him back to life.

For some time afterwards, there were three suns in the sky, and people had three shadows. But the rebellious Makunaima would not follow the trail that Father Sun had marked out for him across the heavens. Father Sun scolded him, and Pia pleaded with him, but this only incited him to more lawless actions. One afternoon, he decided to visit his mother's benab and went so close to the earth that he made the lakes and rivers boil and set the tree tops afire. The next day, all the peoples of the earth complained to Father Sun, and for the first time, the ebony people, who were neighbours of Tihona, made themselves heard. They sent their most important gods to complain to Father Sun: Nyan, the Sky God, who created all things; and his lesser dieties, Earth Mother, Mother of the Rivers, Snake Spirit and Anancy the Spiderman, a god and trickster all in one.

Father Sun called out to the Great Spirit, "Dweller in the Heights, who are these strange gods?"

And the Great Spirit replied, "My Kingdom of the Sky is so vast, there's room for any stranger-god who comes in peace."

So, Nyan, the Sky God, was welcomed by the Great Spirit and they spoke with one voice, describing how the rivers and lakes had become boiling cauldrons, and a million trees so many torches in the wind.

94

remorse. He had promised Father Sun to take his place beside him in the skies when his work on earth was done and he knew that he could never keep his promise now. He called out to Father Sun, trying to explain, and to this day Pia does not know if his father ever heard him.

But the news spread like fire that Pia and Anancy had become brothers, and rills of sparkling water began to sing; Wind strummed the harp-strings of the trees; and people in the Human World, listening, made songless drums sing in time to melodies of flutes and panpipes. Makunaima, skulking in the glooms of forests of the night, made a pact with Mantop, the Sower of Death, and grumbled to himself, promising to destroy this universal happiness.

But Tihona, sitting in her Kingdom of Clouds and Mist, her nimble fingers weaving, smiled, for she had lost one son and gained, for herself, the everlasting gift of making rainbows.

THE COMING OF AMALIVACA
Jan Carew
(Guyana)   Amerindian Legend

My name is Wind and I am lonely. Look on me and
wonder, for now you see me and now you don't. I have
long hair like lianas on the forest trees, and my eyes are
bright as pools mirroring the sun. I can fly faster than
Harpy Eagle and sometimes I soar so high that I sweep
dust and cobwebs from the rafters of Heaven.

For countless moons, I kept my loneliness to myself,
but the day came when I couldn't bear it any longer and
a knot of pain in my heart broke. So I howled through
the valleys, roared across the savannahs and hurled myself like a flight of mad Cruiser Birds through the Pastures
of Heaven. And night and day, I cried out like a Baboon-
mother who had lost her one-child. During this season of
sorrow, I couldn't bear to see my stricken face staring
back at me from quiet lakes and rivers, so, everywhere,
I went I made still water fretful. Because loneliness was
my lot, I searched everywhere for company. I didn't mind
what kind of company it was: the trees that sighed and
leaned away from me; the hot plains that threw dust in
my eyes; the tall grass that hissed like snakes when I
passed by; the spiked stars that pricked my fingers when
I touched them; the cold moon that froze me to the
marrow of my bones; or the hot sun that blistered me in
its furnace heat; all of these I tried in vain to befriend.

So, I was very pleased, one night, when I heard the
echo of drums coming from a village deep in the forest.
I crept up softly-softly until I was close enough to see
what was going on. The people of this village had built
a circle of bright red clay huts in a wide forest clearing

100

and a cluster of drummers sat in the centre of the clearing. I hid in a grove of giant greenheart trees, and as soon as I settled down, chains of dancers trouped out. They pounded the earth with their bare feet in time to the concert of drumming. One drummer, who was tall and straight like a young mora tree and who wore the feathered headdress of a magician, stood up and sang a welcoming chant:

Welcome to the festival of the harvest-moon!
The gods have been kind to us; Aiomon Kondi,
The Great Spirit,
Balanced the seasons of rain and sun
And brought us rich crops
Of corn and cassava
And he promised that he would send us a
Prophet to end strife amongst the earth people.

And I, listening, crept up closer to hear. I wanted to catch every word so that I could take away bright memories to ease my loneliness. The magician sang on,

Welcome to Ichillibar,
The land of the Human Beings . . .

Lurking there in the shadows, I thought to myself, "So these are the Human Beings! I've seen many folks in my time, but I never ran across the Human Beings". And I almost said aloud, "They look like all the other folk on earth to me, except that some have anthracite skin, and cotton eyes and ivory teeth, while others have mahogany skin and blue-black hair and tilted eyes.

"But the way in which they dance is exciting," I had to admit to myself. "They move as if their limbs are messengers sent by the gods to spread joy."

So, listening to the drums and looking at the spectacle of dancers, something inside me stirred and for the first time in my born days I felt that if I joined the Human Beings, if a blood-knot could bind us together forever, then I would never have to be lonely again. I moved closer to the circle of dancers, so close that I could stretch out my hand and touch them as they danced by. They stopped, every now and then, to drink *casheri* from bowls made of dry coconut shells. The drumming was hynotic, and I, keeping time with my foot stirred up a cloud of dust, and leaves in the surrounding trees made such a commotion they seemed to be clapping hands and applauding.

I could not restrain myself any longer and so I joined the dancers, moving along the outer edge of the clearing. And with a single gulp I drank up all the *casheri* in the communal bowl. The drink went to my head, and I danced faster and faster until I became a whirlwind. Before I knew it I had uprooted giant mora and green-heart trees and killed half the Human Beings at Ichillibar. The dead and wounded were strewn around the clearing and I saw the magician with the feathered headdress very gently turning over the bodies so that he could separate the living from the dead.

"It is strange," I told myself. "I wanted so badly to join the Human Beings, but this great strength that I have, which I sometimes cannot control, has made me their enemy!" I sat down on the fallen trees in the gigantic clearing I had made in the forest and would have wept. But I knew that my tears would only fall in cascades and drown the remnants of the Human Beings. I was sober now and wanted to bring them no more sorrow.

The magician with the feathered headdress approached me boldly and said, "You came quietly like a thief, Wind, and without warning brought death and destruction to us, the Human Beings".

"But I only wanted to join you," I said, "I wanted to become a Human Being. I swear by all the gods, and most of all by the Great Spirit, that I did not mean to harm your people. I'll do anything you say to atone for what I have done."

"Anything?" the magician asked.

"Yes, anything," I said.

"Then you must help us find the prophet whom Aiomon Kondi, the Great Spirit, promised to send to us."

"Where will I find this prophet?" I asked.

"Somewhere in the wider world," the magician said, and he touched his feathered plumes and would have vainshed, but I said to him, "Tell me, Magician of the Human Beings, why are you and your people here and how did you get here?"

The magician said, "My ancestors once lived in the Pastures of Heaven, but there came a time when the gods felt that we should inhabit the earth; so, the Great Spirit opened a door in a corner of the sky and my people climbed down a ladder of moonbeams, until they came to this place which is called Ichillibar, the Place of the Chosen People. The Great Spirit sent us here, so that we could set an example to all men of how to live in harmony and peace; but ever since the first ancestor set foot on earth, we have been at war with our neighbours, and fighting endless wars we ourselves have become corrupted. This is why the Great Spirit promised he would send a prophet to us. For this prophet, he said, would end strife amongst the Earth people." The magician would say no more and he touched his feathered headdress and vanished.

After the magician disappeared, I noticed that the air was still and the sun felt like burning fire on my back. I did not know where to turn for help. Here was I wanting so badly to become one of the Human Beings and yet I had brought nothing but disaster to them, and now I had to go in search of a prophet to redeem them. And if I found their prophet, then, perhaps, I too would be redeemed. I knew that without clues it was no use wandering around the earth in search of a prophet, so I sat very still pondering. The drops of sweat that fell from my troubled brow flowed into a nearby creek and helped to water the dry plains. When, wearied with the weight of much thinking, I began to doze off in the hot sun, Tupi, the vampire who is the chief messenger of the Great Spirit, came and shook me by the shoulder.

"Wake up, Wind," Tupi said, "for I have come to summon you. The Great Spirit, my master, is angry after he saw what you did to the Human Beings at Ichillibar."

My first impulse was to run away, to hide somewhere in the great wastes of the forests or the seas, but I restrained myself.

"I would prefer not to come now," I said to Tupi. "I cannot face the anger of the Great Spirit. My soul is bruised and I would need time to compose my thoughts, before I face him."

"My master says that you must come, at once, Wind."

"I'll not come," I declared and I rushed away fleeing across forests and mountains and deserts and oceans, and finally, when I was so weary that I could not keep my own head up, I fell asleep on the flat top of a red mountain called Roraima which is the sacred mountain of the Human Beings. But while I was asleep, Tupi, the messenger of the Great Spirit, crept up the mountainside and bound me hand and foot with lianas. He then carried me on his back to the cave where the Great Spirit lives. Tupi threw me down on the floor of the cave. I woke up and slowly it began to dawn on me that I was in the house of Aiomon Kondi. Tupi had vanished but the Great Spirit sat on his gigantic throne of quartz and his single eye shone like a conflagration.

"Why did you try to escape when I summoned you?" the Great Spirit asked.

And I stuttered and could find no answer.

"I spent a sleepless night thinking about your misdeeds, Wind. Why did you inflict so much pain on the Human Beings?" the Great Spirit continued. "I will tell you why

104

you are lonely Wind. You are lonely because all that you have in your heart is loneliness. You have no love in your heart and I, the Great Spirit, measure all men by their shadows and by their love."

And whilst he was speaking, I could not bear to face his furnace-eye and looked away. He ordered Tupi to set me free and as if he sprung from the earth under me, the vampire-messenger appeared and cut the lianas with which he had bound me. I shook the aches out of my limbs and flexed my muscles, and for the first time I could look all around me. The cave was deep and wide and at the mouth was a waterfall. The walls of the gorge, into which the water tumbled, were lined with hosts of orchids.

Sun came out suddenly as though anxious to find out what sentence the Great Spirit would pass on me, and without warning, Rainbow appeared at the mouth of the cave. She was combing her hair and making a garland for herself out of orchids. As soon as my eyes made four with hers, something happened to me that had never happened before in my life. I began to sing. The trees leaned forward to listen; the tall grass on the savannah sighed; and the running brooks took up the melodies and carried them down mountainsides into the wide streams and out towards the seas and valleys of the deep.

The Aiomon Kondi said, "Wind, you have all along been so obsessed with your own loneliness that, without knowing it, you have harmed the Human Beings, over and over again. Why have you been so heartless? The Human Beings complain that sometimes on your way, to or from the sea, you tear off the roofs of their huts, choke them with dust, destroy their fields of corn and cassava, and, as if that is not enough, they say that there are times when you herd dark clouds together and drown them with a deluge of rain, and then you use the raindrops like

105

whips to chastise them. What have you got to say for yourself?"

I was speechless. How could I have inflicted this suffering upon the Human Beings without even knowing it!

"When I summoned you, here, I had made up my mind to banish you to a cave and to seal up the entrance with a giant boulder," Aiomon Kondi continued, "but now that I have heard you sing, I've changed my mind. So, as long as I live, and as long as the earth and skies live, you must make music wherever you go. I will put harp-strings on the forest trees, panpipes in the tall savannah grass and melodious tongues in the springs and the singing brooks sweet and I will bury drums in the depths of the sea so that everytime you pass by they can resurrect themselves. So go now, Wind, and walk well!"

I wanted to tell the Great Spirit that it was Rainbow who had given me the gift of song and music, to confess that I nursed a secret hope of marrying her, but I kept all this to myself. I feared that he would banish me to the end of the earth where I would never see Rainbow again.

So I asked instead, "Tell me, Great Spirit, where will I find the prophet whom the Human Beings would have me bring to them?"

"You will find the prophet of the Human Beings sooner than you think, Wind," the Great Spirit said; and he would say no more.

I left the cave of the Great Spirit and walked out into the morning light. Rainbow was plaiting orchids into her hair and I plucked up my courage and said, "I like your hairstyle, Lady of the Waterfall."

She smiled and said to me quietly, "What is the sea like?"

I did not know why she asked this question, at this particular time, but I replied by singing her this song:

The first time I saw the sea,
I did not know
it was green like parrots,
blue, as a buck-crab's back,
black as a marudi's wing.
The first time I heard the sea,
it spoke differently
to rivers
and trees.
The first time I saw the sea,
it licked my feet with a rough tongue,
grained with sand like an ocelot's.
And the sea said to me:
Wide the world wide, Wind!
Wide and deep, Wind!
Wide the world wide, Wind!
Wider than the heart can see, Wind!
Wide the world wide, Wind!

And Rainbow looked at me and said, "No one's ever made the sea so wild and beautiful for me before."

I was so pleased that my natural shyness left me and I reached out and touched her. But when I tried to get closer to her, her hair became tangled in the nearby rocks and Sun, looking on, became jealous and hiding behind a cloud, sent a flight of swallows to throw a shadow-cloak around Rainbow. I tried to follow her but she vanished up a staircase of mist and filtered sunlight.

I never tried to get close to Rainbow, again after that, but I sang songs to her, as I went from country to country, in search of the prophet of the Human Beings.

One morning, bright with dew and singing birds, Tupi, the messenger of Aiomon Kondi, woke me up and said, "I have news for you, Wind."

"News? So far, you've only brought me bad news, Tupi. What have I done now?"

"Rainbow is with child, your child. She said that if you

107

want to share the child, when it is born, you must scoop out a cradle on top of Roraima, the Red Mountain, and wait. For before the horned moon visits the night sky, again, she will bring the child to you."

That very day, I went to the top of Roraima and sculpted a cradle out of the red earth, and lined it with young and tender tamarind leaves, and planted stunted palms to shade it from the sun, and then I waited. I did not have to wait long, for one afternoon, Rainbow brought the baby-boy and set him down in the cradle. In my eagerness to thank her, I scattered the mists around Roraima and she vanished.

I named the boy-child Amalivaca, "the child of my searching". Amalivaca was a bright-eyed black boy with a voice full of singing. When Aiomon Kondi sent Tupi, his messenger, to be the boy's companion, I knew that he would grow up to be one of the chosen ones.

Tupi was ugly. He had dark, lack-lustre wings, a sharp, pointed mouth and mournful, smoky eyes, and his voice was more unmelodious than a crow's. But Tupi had a wise heart and he was kind and patient.

Amalivaca's companions were condors and eagles who took him for rides on their backs, so that he could see the whole world spreading out below him; or the condors and the eagles would sit in a feathered circle and tell him stories about the shape of the world and the mysteries of people and of all things great and small that lived according to the harmonies of earth and water and fire. Tupi, on the other hand, told him tales of his journeys down the River of Night, where the souls of the living and the dead beat their bats' wings against the still air and chant poem-hymns to the gods.

I taught Amalivaca how to sing. And when the rains came and water cascaded down to the valleys below Roraima, the running tongues of brooks and rivulets carried his songs everywhere.

Rainbow always came to Amalivaca, in the daytime, riding the mists and the clouds, as if they were wild horses, and she wove garments for him out of many colours and studded them with fireflies and stars.

I would have liked Amalivaca to live on that friendly mountain-top, forever, but the day came when Aiomon Kondi, summoned Tupi, and when Tupi returned to the Red Mountain he said, "The time has come for Amalivaca to go to Ichillibar, the Place of the Human Beings. You wronged the Human Beings, Father Wind, and your son must make peace with them."

And Amalivaca flung his arms around Tupi's neck, and tears, falling on the vampire's lack-lustre wings, shone like jewels.

"You must go, boy, you must go," Tupi kept saying, and his smoky eyes were sad.

And I pounded my fists against the cliff side and cried out, "Great Spirit, let my one-boy live free on Roraima; he inherited Rainbow's brightness; his heart is soft as a hummingbird's wing; and he knows neither hate nor evil!"

Aiomon Kondi spoke from the depths of the sacred cave, and his voice sounded like drums, "Only Amalivaca, the boy with Rainbow's brightness, can bring peace and harmony to the Human Beings. Let him go, Father Wind. He has inherited your gift of music; so give to him in addition the magic to strum the harp-strings on the trees and to turn the tall grass on the savannahs into panpipes."

I did what the Great Spirit commanded, and then I took my son, Amalivaca, down to the valley and left him in a grove of wild mango trees, where the earth was carpeted with blossoms. After I said goodbye to him, he sat on the earth, and taking out the magic panpipe I gave him, began to play the tunes I had taught him. The nearby creek picked up the tunes and carried them through the forest, and greedy flocks of birds abandoned

109

trees heavy with fruit to gather round him and listen; and after a while all living things, men, reptiles, insects and all the wild brute-beasts, came as close as they could to the wild mango grove.

So, Amalivaca, the man-child of Wind and Rainbow, became the Prophet, not only of the Human Beings but of all living things. And for the first time since the Snake God had stirred under the sea and raised the earth on his back, Amalivaca, the Prophet, brought peace and harmony to the world.

TIMU AND THE KUNAIMA
Aubrey Williams

(Guyana)   Amerindian Legend

This is the story as it is told among the Warrou to this day:

It is said that when the blood first came from the cradle of new life in the body of Timu, she was already shaped as a woman and desirable, and the day after her mother had annointed her body and brought her out after the rights of puberty, the youth Moluk, who was tall with the strength of a man, came forward from the crowd and held the nipple of her left breast to claim her. But Timu did not insert her finger in the hole of her navel, and Moluk knew he was refused. Everybody was ashamed and sad for Moluk and avoided one another's eyes. But it was so, and Moluk hoped that in his second or third attempt at claiming Timu, he might be successful.

It was a time when the Warrou was strong. The Carib was broken and scattered in the rivers and the Warrou had claimed most of the hills of the North West. The land yielded much cassava and maize; the game was good and of many numbers; and there was much laughter heard among the tribe. The feathers of the Warrou Arrow were feared throughout the lands to North West and the men had time to dream and to make beautiful things with their hands from out of their dreams.

After Moluk had failed for the third time with Timu, it was already a year since he first claimed her. So, he demanded the name of his rival that he might gamble or fight for her. But Timu had said that there was no rival, and Moluk was soon known among the tribe as the silent one.

Then one day, a warrior named Tiho returned to the people of Hosororo with a strange tale. He said he had tracked a tapir, from the foot of the hill of Maridowa, up into the virgin forest and out into the swamps, behind the hill, towards the blue mountains. And at the time of day when he stood upon the shadow of himself, he had suddenly come upon the carcass of the tapir lying in the bizzy-bizzy reed. The carcass was grey, and when he had cut the flesh of its throat, it was seen that the meat had no blood. After he had told this story to the Chief, and the Wise One who sat in the Chief's shadow, the one who conversed with Makunaima the Star Spinner, the Wise One took the cayman tooth that hung from his neck and with the cayman tooth scribed a square on the earth before him. It was the first time the Wise One had ever done this within Warrou memory. His face held the pallor of death, and turning to the Chief, the Wise One said, "This is the commencement of bad times, for the Kunaima is with us." And the wind blew for three days with great force, uprooting trees, breaking the stalks of maize, and cassava, and many huts were flattened. The rivers grew muddy and salty, and a sickness took hold of the people. The Wise One fasted and conversed with Makunaima, but the sun increased its heat and many hills took fire. So, the land changed and became strange. The women grew thin; the bellies of the children swelled; the men became bright-eyed and sullen; and there was no longer the sound of laughter and music among the Warrou. In the hunt, the warriors increasingly came upon white blood-drained meat of the Kunaima-kill; such meat could never be eaten.

The game seemed to have deserted the forest, and there were no bird songs, save the voice of the hoarse vulture, and the naked necked Condor. The Warrou took to eating snakes and toads and wood pulp and insects.

One quiet dark night, when the weak cries of the hungry children could be heard on the hill of Hosororo, Timu heard her name called outside her mother's hut in a strange voice. Her mother was ill. She lay in her hammock in a coma of exhaustion, breathing heavily. The voice called again, and as though in a dream, Timu went from her hammock into the night.

Timu had gone to the Kunaima. This was the first time. It was strange. Bemused in a heavy dream, as it

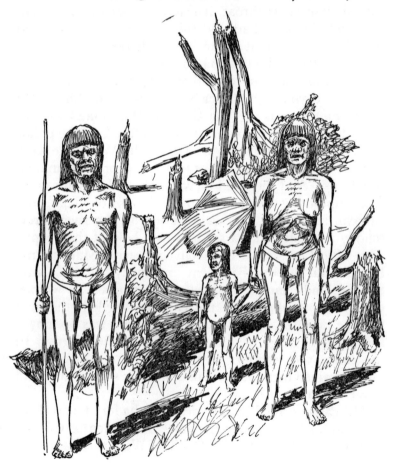

were, Timu walked towards the burning green eyes, deep
in the black forest. Her singing, intoxicating joy was
mounting with each step. She was hypnotized by the
beckoning, all seeing, glowing green Kunaima-eyes. The
hot, strong arms held her, as the Anaconda holds, but
with a perfumed heat that jangled her senses. Yet her
consciousness was full and sharp. She could feel the damp,
dead leaves against her back and the tremor of the
muscles of her opening thighs. The green eyes enveloped
her in a phosphorous of storms; in her nose was the smell
of all the blossoms of the forest when the moon is full;
in her head was thunder of water. Her body strained to
open itself and to give and to hold.

There is a saying among the Warrou, which goes:
"And she who receives the latex of the Kunaima, in an
embrace of love. . . ."

The next day, the earth was cool. There was a bright,
pearly light and then the rains came. The rain washed
the land of its misery, and revitalized everything; the
birds sang; the flowers were everywhere; the Aruka
became full and black, and the fish broke its surfrace as
before. The game returned from the jungle to the forest;
the people smiled and planted cassava and maize. There
was no message of the bad times in the new songs of the
Warrou.

And Timu, the one who had received the latex of the
Kunaima in the embrace of love! Within a month her
belly swelled as though she were on the brink of child-
bed; so she was to remain for the balance of her life.

It was at this time that Tiho, the hunter, the observer
of life, began to form the song of Timu and the Kunaima,
the song that I tell you now as it is told among the
Warrou.

Within the new wave of life in the tribe of the
Warrou, Moluk took unto himself as wife, a ripe widow
who had long hungered for him, and in the glory of his

115

children's laughter forgot to feel his love for Timu; and Timu walked among the Warrou with her big Kunaima-belly, never ageing for twenty years.

It was a time of drought again, but of normal intensity, so that only the forest was worried, and the Who-You? birds called in the daytime. In the second month of this drought, Timu the ageless of the big belly felt the pangs of birth descend upon her, and took to her hammock. A murmuring tremor seemed to pass through the tribe and the waiting was general. Tiho added a new stanza to his long song, while Moluk, in a state of daily premonition and dejection, was specially tender towards his family.

For one month, Timu lay in her hammock of labour. The river was again salty; the game was scarce; the cassava roots were small and the maize shoots were barely spotted with grain. Yet, all attention lay heavily upon the state of Timu in her labour, for though it was not stated by open mouth, the tribe seemed to feel that therein their fate lay. This was indeed a tense time for the good Warrou people. For it's said among the Warrou that she who receives the latex of the Kunaima. . . . All seemed to know of this saying. All seemed to share the strange prolonged agony of Timu, though none, save Moluk, spoke or told of this fear. The Wise One, who was now very old and wiser, conversed daily with Makunaima. The moon of that month had already starved itself to a sliver of silver and only came out in shame, a little before dawn for air. In such a night, before the shamefaced, thin moon had shown itself, Timu heard her name called by a strange voice out of the darkness. New strength entered her limbs. She left her hammock and walked into the night towards the river, towards the low, salt, muddy Aruka.

Now, it will be very difficult to tell all that happened before the dawn. Even when I'm finished, I know it will

116

be badly stated, but I will tell of it. I will try to tell it all.

Timu took the path along the bank of the river, until she reached the creek whose banks are made of the old shells of shell-fish, though the sea was many miles away in flight even for a Condor. When she reached the creek, she walked in and washed herself in the shallow, salty water. While she rubbed her body with her long hair, the sick, weak moon showed itself and the pangs of birth descended upon her. As you know, this was no natural birth. Her body seemed possessed by the great snake itself. Her limbs moved as though they didn't belong to her. Her ankles entwined themselves behind her neck, while her hands squeezed the life out of her belly. "The Kunaima-birth is always a male child that grows to manhood, before it is dry . . . !" so goes the saying. Her pelvis broke and her birth lay before her; it glowed in the dark and she could see it; she was broken but yet alive. "When the Kunaima-birth attains manhood, it rapes and strangles its mother and goes to the forest to be slain by its father, the Kunaima!" This is in the story, and this started to happen. As the Kunaima-birth grew before her, Timu could not get her legs down from behind her neck, for the cradle of life within her was broken. The Kunaima-birth attained manhood before her, and yet she could not get her legs down.

In her waning senses, Timu could see the Kunaima-birth was, indeed, the Kunaima itself. The Kunaima-birth placed its strong hands on Timu's throat. Holding and squeezing it, it pulled its standing self into Timu's broken, mutilated body as her eyes pulped from their sockets and her tongue strained from its roots, clenched in her teeth. This is as it is told, and so I tell you now. And the Kunaima-birth stood away from the mangled pulp that was Timu, now unrecognizable, and walked blindly into the forest. It was nearly dawn. The wind rose; the clouds of the rains and storms claimed the uplands; lightning ravaged the blackness; and thunders shook the earth. The Kunaima-birth, never dry, now wet with rain, stood in the forest and waited in the wild storm. And in the storm, in the noise of the wind and the thunder and the trees, there began to be wild Kunaima-laughter.

The emotions of the earth, the sky and the wind entered the Warrou of the hill and they came from their houses into the wind and the rain. The Wise One was conversing with Makunaima in a frenzy and beating a drum. His face, parallel to the earth, gazing into the storm and into the forest, the Kunaima claimed his new son with Death and laughter. For the kill, the Kunaima took the form of the Bushmaster. The Kunaima-birth stood beneath the huge Mora tree which is beside the Hosororo falls to this day. And the Kunaima, in the form of the coiled Bushmaster, struck, so that when the fangs entered the neck of the Kunaima-birth, the Kunaima-birth screamed with the voice of Timu. And the people of the hill heard and knew, and the rain stayed for two weeks, and the times softened, and the broken body of Timu was washed by the swollen Aruka, far, far, into the big water of the sea. And the Condors ate the dead flesh of the Kunaima-birth, and the Warrou repaired their life and stood up, and after a time, there was again laughter, and Tiho the poet, the observer, the one who laughed at all things, sang the song of Timu and the Kunaima.

A HOME BENEATH THE CLOUDS
Roy Heath

(Guyana)   Amerindian Legend

There was famine in the sky. The cassava plants, stricken
with blight, had small tubers at harvesting time and most
of the game had fled. Even the wild orange trees, which
abounded in the region, had withered leaves. The women,
whose duty it was to go out in search of roots and grubs,
had to wander farther afield, on each occasion returning
with less than the time before.

The chiefs of the Meenao clan had met the day before
to discuss what was to be done to avoid disaster, but
could not agree on a course of action; and those who
believed that a long trek should be undertaken were now
huddled together around the fire.

"We must leave now!" exclaimed Isiari. "The women
bring back little and the men find no game."

"Weak men want to remain; they are afraid of the
journey to new lands," another chief taunted those who
were in favour of putting off the trip.

"We will come back when the famine is over," said
another chief.

Isiari's leadership was acknowledged on account of the
fact that the numbers in his village had increased since
his predecessor's death.

"The savannah is sick," he warned the company.

"If we go, what will happen to the crop of cassava we
just planted?" asked a chief who had not yet spoken.

"We must know what to do and do it now," warned
Isiari. "Your cassava will rot and you will reap a harvest
of dust."

And so discussion went on, until the moon fell below

119

the mountains; but nothing had yet been decided.

In the end, Isiari declared that he would take the people of his village in search of new lands. He would return, when the moon began to waste away, to report what he had found.

Isiari informed the villagers of the chief's indecision and disclosed his own plan. Agreement among the men was almost unanimous: the day after the next, the inhabitants of the village would set out towards the North.

The following day the women collected their gourds, their *matapees, warishis* and cassava graters, while the men gathered their bows, arrows, firesticks and their most prized possessions of all, the smooth-ground stone axes.

The *piaiman* had been up before everyone else, arranging the pebbles and objects with which he called up the spirits that caused sickness. Not only must he be careful not to leave anything behind, but he had to make a suitable container for transporting them.

Finally, the men went out to their garden place to harvest what they could of the blighted cassava, uprooting the immature plants and stripping them of their hardly swollen roots.

By mid-afternoon the sun had driven everyone to seek shelter under the large hut. The *piaiman* sought out the chief and asked him to come to his own hut, and the two men left at once, followed by the gaze of those who were not sleeping.

"We must not go, tomorrow!" exclaimed the *paiman,* addressing the chief, who had followed him into his hut.

"Why?"

"We cannot go. Death will set out with us on the journey."

"Death will come to us, if we do not go," the chief reminded him.

The *piaiman* did not reply, but went to the corner of the hut, where he took a pebble from among a collection of objects in a box made of cane and fibre. He held it in his outstretched right hand, as if to keep it as far away from himself as he possibly could. The chief took the smooth, blue-veined stone, and before he could examine it, felt its unusual warmth and a surface covered with a viscous fluid. On stepping outside, he saw that the pebble was oozing blood and that his fingers were red, as when he dipped them in the carcass of a newly-slain bush-hog. Isiari, disturbed by the portent, returned the pebble to the *piaiman* with an angry gesture and turned away in the direction of the big hut.

The *piaiman* ran after him. "We cannot go!" he urged the chief.

"We must go! If you utter a word to. . . ."

"You are afraid," the *piaiman* interrupted him.

Isiari turned away once more and left the *piaiman* holding the pebble.

At night, around a large fire lit outside the big hut, the inhabitants of the village danced and chanted improvised songs:

> "At the wasting of the moon
> We will come back
> To the land where our roots swell
> And the sky is never thirsty."

When the caiman began to bark, the singing stopped and the villagers lay down to sleep, surrounded by the panting stillness of the night.

The next day, at sunrise, a column of people was moving along the thick clouds, where the once lush grass was now parched and lifeless. At the head of the column Isiari and the *piaiman* were striding side by side, while the women with small children and one pregnant woman were at the rear.

The column strung out and the gaps between groups became larger until, towards mid-day, those at the back were no longer able to see the leading group.

Late in the afternoon, Dunoo, the pregnant woman, saw the villagers gathered together in one spot and she believed that they were waiting for her. But, on approaching, her attention was drawn to the chief and the *piaiman*, who, stretched full length on the ground, were looking through a gap in the clouds. There was great excitement among those standing around. The men had laid their bows and arrows on the ground and were awaiting their chance to see for themselves the sights the chief was describing. Below them were deer, bush-hog and *labba* on the banks of the creeks, and in the distance the savannah had been inundated by recent rains.

By sunset, everyone had caught a glimpse of the world below. Some of the men set out in search of a large tree with lianas which might be joined to form a rope long enough to reach the ground below while the women made a fire and warmed the cassava cakes they had brought with them.

The *piaiman* could not still his anxieties at the proposed descent into the new world. He and the chief talked at length about going down to the grass-lands and forests where, for all they knew, unseen dangers lurked. But they agreed that it was too late to prevent the villagers from exploring the place.

That same night when the stars thronged together like phosphorescent leaves, the villagers embarked, one by one, on the long descent; at first, the chief, followed by the *piaiman* and the other men, and finally the women.

But when Dunoo, the pregnant women, held on to the rope and lowered herself carefully through the gap, her swollen belly became wedged in the folds of surrounding cloud. Although she cried out, no one heard her, and in the darkness no one saw her plight. She struggled to free herself until her limbs grew numb and her head drooped to one side in sleep.

The next morning, Dunoo's husband, who had waited

in vain for her to come down, climbed back up to assist her. First, he tried to insert his hands between Dunoo and the cloud, in order to widen the breach; then he pulled her towards him. But his efforts were unavailing. He climbed down once more, resolved to wait at the foot of the rope for the first sign of the clouds dispersing.

The villagers of the Meenao clan left to go in search of a suitable place to spend the night. By a bend in a river, they made a camp and the next day built a large benab of stout posts from saplings felled with their stone axes.

That night, Death, who had accompanied the villagers, unknown to them, hoisted himself up the rope and killed the child-big woman. Her husband, waiting on the ground below, felt blood dripping on his head and believed it was raining. "Tomorrow," he said to himself, "the clouds will move and Dunoo will be able to come down."

But when tomorrow came, Dunoo was still wedged between the clouds. Her husband, tired of waiting, went away in disgust to find his fellow clansmen.

At his approach, the women and children ran to hide, believing that his blood-smeared head belonged to an unknown creature of the new lands. On the return of the men from hunting, the women told them of the red-headed animal that had come to the village. Thereupon the men went to benab and killed their clansman. But the victim's brother recognised him and buried him in a sitting position, as was the custom of his clan.

The *piaiman* reminded the chief of his warning that Death would accompany them. Convinced that the *piaiman* had been right, the chief asked him what they ought to do.

"It is too late to go back now," the *piaiman* answered. "Let us wait until the agreed time."

And so, the villagers stayed in their temporary home hunting the abundant game and gathering what grew

124

beneath the ground and on the trees. But they did not plant cassava, since their stay was too short for the roots to swell for eating.

One man found a way to stun the fish in the river with the sap of a plant that grew near the benab, while another learned to imitate the calls of the birds and lure them near enough to be shot with an arrow.

And the moon went on waning with each succeeding night, until the time approached for the villagers to leave their temporary home beneath the sky.

The men left on a final hunt, after which they smoked the carcasses of deer and bush-hog to take back with them as evidence of the land's abundance. And the *piaiman,* who was tempted to tell his clansmen of the bleeding pebble and the presence of Death in their midst, kept silent. There was enough time to dissuade them and the chiefs of other villages from making the journey again.

On the morning of their going away, the villagers gathered in front of the benab to wait for a signal from the chief who would lead them back to their old home, as he had brought them to this. The women's *warishis,* laden with roots and fruit, rested on their arched backs. Their children, whose young skin glistened as a result of regular feeding, stood around, some holding dried fish and others with *warishis* and other household goods under their arms.

The company set off behind the chief and the *piaiman,* leaving the river behind them; and as they turned eastwards, where the rope lay, a storm broke.

"If it is raining in the sky," the *piaiman* thought, "the famine will be over and there would be no need to tell them about the pebble."

In the end, the villagers of the Meenao clan arrived at the place where the rope was dangling from the sky. The chief, as leader of his people, made the ascent first. All being well he would tug on the rope when he reached the top, so that the others might follow him.

Soon he had disappeared in the rain that obscured the villagers' view of the clouds. The *piaiman,* unable to bear the suspense of waiting, was about to follow him when the clouds were rent by a sheet of lightning that showed the chief at the top of the rope grasping two legs above him.

Dunoo's clansmen, seduced by the bounty of the new lands, had forgotten her. The chief came down and told them that she was dead and furthermore, that her swollen belly still blocked the path to their home. There was nothing left for them but to wait for a break in the clouds, however long it took.

And thus the children of the Meenao clan, who once lived in the sky, came to inhabit the land beneath the sky. They still point in awe to the area where Dunoo was caught, and declare that she can often be seen struggling to free herself.

THE LEGEND OF GUAGUGIONA
Christopher Laird
(Trinidad and Tobago)   Legend

Guagugiona woke up one morning, or should I say his eyes opened, for he was not awake as you and I are when the sun's rays reach above the horizon and bid with sleep for our waking. His eyes opened but his mind did not wonder from object to object around the room, from the cooking utensils, to his wife, to the doorway, to the sun. No. He was like a man possessed. He had one thing in his head and saw only that; the things around him were only shadows in his body like those haunting the limbs of a blind man.

During the night the goddess Biju had visited him and spoken of his affliction. He couldn't remember how she spoke; he couldn't remember the words, but she told him things that had been written in his being but which he had never noticed. She had showed him himself as he was, breaking into the sores of Yaya, possessed of the seed of destruction which would poison generations to come. She had shown him his people, breaking out in eruptions of discontent and foolish ambition, gathering themselves into a tight circle of confusion that would fly apart and vanish into loneliness like the stars on a moonlight night.

All these things he had seen clearly but what was more important she had shown him what had to be done to save himself and his people. This is what he held in his mind as he swung himself out of his hammock and, as was his custom, sat on his mat against the West wall to await the food his wife was preparing for him. Biju's instructions were very drastic: the tribe was to be split down the middle, one half remaining; the other half, with him as leader, was to come to her. Guagugiona thought of the

127

task ahead of him in convincing the council and obtaining their co-operation and the support of the people. Though to you and me the task would have seemed impossible for one man to achieve, Guagugiona was not worried. He thought of the vision he had received and it didn't occur to him that he should fail, so he was not worried.

He was so engrossed in thought that he didn't notice when his wife accidentally dropped some of the cassava cakes on the floor and stooped to pick them up with a quick apprehensive look in his direction. He received the food and fed himself without looking, his eyes staring beyond the walls, beyond the town, beyond the shore, to the horizon.

When he had had his fill, he took the rest of the cakes and wrapping them into his belt, he set off to the council lodge, striding through the town noticing no greeting and not hearing himself talking aloud the thoughts that ran through his head. Women sitting in the doorways ran to grab their children from his whirlwind path. Men came out of their houses hastily tying their belts and hurried toward the council lodge after an awed glance at the resolute Guagugiona.

When he arrived under the roof of the council lodge, Guagugiona immediately began talking to those who had arrived. When everyone had arrived and were seated Guagugiona repeated his story. His listeners took in the blank glaze of his eyes, the assured manner and the matter of fact voice that delivered this message from the gods. They looked at Guagugiona and thought of the Guagugiona of yesterday, the Guagugiona they all knew: a flamboyant man, a bit of a dandy, full of jokes and charm but one who in the thick of battle became silent and ruthless as he carved his way through the enemies' ranks; a man who didn't normally take the council meetings seriously, making fun of the pompous and gifted with a sense of irony in his own speeches, but a man who on occasions in the past had become grimly determined to steer the council to actions that often headed off disasters that none had foreseen.

Yes, there is no doubt about it, Guagugiona was a contradictory sort of character, but a man that held the respect of almost all the people and was considered to have inherited many of the talents of his father who had been a great Bisiri.*

They looked at him again and saw a Guagugiona they had never seen. A man as serious and as determined as he had ever been, but one who remained detached from the proceedings and whose actions as he undid the cassava cakes from his belt and ate them through his words, exhibited the irony that his tongue had parcelled on previous occasions. But they didn't laugh. For as he spoke and as the story repeated itself in many ways, his eyes seemed to grow in brightness; his actions became more co-ordinated; his voice gathered strength and soon he was beating the hearts of all who were there as the riddles he had begun with molded themselves into a poem which his searing gaze soldered to the souls of his listeners.

Not that there weren't those who accused him of madness or of trying to draw attention to himself; there were, but their words had little effect as their accusations were founded, as all there knew, in jealousy and rancour; their wives were known admirers of Guagugiona. The bitter and spiteful words spoken by these objectors, in fact, helped Guagugiona's cause more than hindered it. Their pettiness was in such contrast to the magnificence of Guagugiona's speech and the significance of his words that they seemed to bestow authority to what he had to say and served even to illustrate the forces of dissent that Biju had mentioned.

* Bisiri — Sage and sorcerer

129

By the time Guagugiona strode out of the council lodge, all the town knew what had happened in the discussion and now he walked back through the town greeting and being greeted by everyone. The whole town seemed to gather in the central square where already fires were being lit and food being prepared for what was to be the most significant gathering of the people in living memory. For it was there that it was made known that the instructions of Biju would be followed to the letter and the people must ready themselves for the sacrifice that they were to make. A sacrifice that would be sung about for generations to come, but one, which if they refused to carry out, would sentence them to a slow and total death.

Two months later, a large canoe could be seen leaving the shore. The lagoon was unusually deserted for that time of day but there were many people on the beach, all looking at the slowly departing boat.

The boat was like a large war canoe with a roofed area in the centre. In the boat were all the women of the town; on the shore were all the men. Guagugiona looked back from the stern oar which he manned and saw the mourning and bewildered gathering of men on the shore even before the sound of their sighs came over the smooth surface of the lagoon. Those on the boat also looked back and some sobbed and there were tears in the eyes of many.

Guagugiona did not cry; he did not smile with satisfaction either; he was serious. He thought of the task ahead and by his example urged the paddlers to put more effort into their work. Soon the boat slid out of the lagoon into the open sea.

He left in the late afternoon. As he threaded his way through the canoes returning after a day's fishing, he waved at those who hailed him. Gradually as he grew further away, the sounds of the town grew fainter. Now

130

the only sounds were those of his paddle in the water:
Dip, pull! Dip, pull! The water slapped and gurgled past
the prow, as Tamusi bent forward putting all his being
behind each pull that hauled him further from land.
Before his eyes he held the image of his father as he was
a year ago when he told the story of Guagugiona.

Everyone knew the story; it was that sort of story, but
the younger ones gaped and the older ones nodded in
deep appreciation as Yolokon Tamulu continued on his
spellbinding way:

Guagugiona and the women travelled many, many
days and nights to the South in search of the goddess
Biju, when, one afternoon, a storm gathering in the East,
rolled down on the party. Almost everyone hurried to
huddle under the shelter; only those on the paddles stayed
glued to the gunwales stabbing at the white fangs of the
angrily leaping waves, Guagugiona, at the stern, was
worried; he saw that this was no ordinary storm and the
loaded boat would have to be very lucky to come through
it in one piece. He ordered four of the women to assist
in baling; as he spoke, a sudden blast ripped the roof off
the shelter exposing the occupants who huddled closer
together in the bottom of the boat. The wind howled and
the rain lashed their bent backs in seeming fury at their
trespass. The boat flew before the storm's onslaught. It
was all Guagugiona could do to keep it on an even keel
as he wrestled with the stern oar. Many in the boat
prayed to Orehu, or sea mother, to save them, others
to thundering Sosyeve to ease his fury.

All prayers seemed to be of no avail as darkness fell.
Each soul was driven in on to itself in the deep darkness
of the storm. They each returned to their wombs as they
crouched in a hurried hiding place from the wrath of
furious parents.

Tonight will be clear, thought Tamusi; the moon will

be full and the sea will glisten as it rolls its smooth back like a huge jellyfish. The sky will be blue with ghost-like clouds standing in it. There may even be rings like monochrome rainbows around the moon, like the rings a pebble forms when it is tossed into a still pond. On nights like these, whether you are travelling on the sea with your back and moving arms reflecting silver and the dew on your prow streaming like Orehu's tears, or you are encamped upon some deserted shore and the water's lips sigh accompanying the waving of the trees overhead as they seek to shield the moonlight from your tired eyes, you forget that other world beneath the waves that threatens on stormy days. You dream of home and a comforting fireside.

The fire surged upward as new wood caught and blazed. The light flickered across Yolokon Tamulu's face as he glanced at the intent faces around him. All was silent save for the crackling and bursting of the wood in the fire. He almost smiled before he continued.

Guagugiona was back on the battlefield. Stinging darts of water struck at his face as he faced the storm grimly. His firm grip on the storm oar (the child that leads the mother) bullied the boat through the waves. The boat gained speed as if under some unkown force; the wind blazed past Guagugiona's ears; the rain scorched his eyes, choked his mouth when suddenly, held in a furious flash of lightning he saw mountains looming at them. Too late, he leant all his weight on the oar; the boat rammed a reef and, mounting it, drove itself onwards to a series of rocks that grew larger than the mountains in their world.

Struggling in the water's treacherous embrace, Guagugiona helped the women to safety above the waterline on the shore beyond the rocks. When everyone was safe, they grew silent within themselves and were conscious only of the gasps, sobs and sighs that ran through them and burst out onto the sand. Gradually, they fell asleep. Guagugiona, exhausted but thankful that the first trial was over, allowed his eyes to close and his breath to slow until he slept.

The next morning, they awoke with the warming sun and gathered themselves around to find that by some miracle, which they could attribute to their prayers, they were all safe. The beach they were on was small; there were cliffs rising around them except where a small stream was crossing the sand; there, there was a narrow ravine that promised access to the interior.

Guagugiona led the party up the ravine, until they emerged on a plain. From there, they saw that the island was dominated by a massive volcano, which every now and again, gave off a stream of vapour. During the next few months, the party explored the island (as indeed they found it was) completely, and founded a town on the other side near the sea but on a small hill as is the custom. Guagugiona had divided them into three groups: one group would assist in constructing a small boat, for Guagugiona was still intent on continuing his quest; another group would hunt, fish and otherwise provide the others with food; while the third group set about establishing the town and taking care of the domestic arrangements. A full year after they had arrived, Guagugiona set off once more, this time alone.

That's what he was doing now, on his own. Repeating the voyage of Guagugiona, on his own. His father had died three months ago, and that, face flickering by firelight, flushed by the sun at evening, had vanished and had become but a mask they had buried. That fireside scene had died, its glowing embers in his heart and the smell of the smoke in his nostrils remained to stoke a cold memory on an open sea.

A lot had happened over the last year. News of a

strange white-skinned people with beards and boats with wings, stories of other peoples being enslaved and of the curious weapons and creatures these strange men brought, had stirred the young people of the town, and they demanded action of the elders. But they had been ignored. The news had been disregarded as lies or as not their affair. Tamusi's father had understood his frustration, and this understanding had restrained him; but with the death of Yolokon Tamulu and with the blessing of his mother, he decided to leave the town and seek answers in the path of his hero, Guagugiona.

He was all alone now to follow Guagugiona down the thread of islands to the South. To Kairi off the coast of the continent of Guania. Guagugiona had arrived at Kairi covered with the sores of his illness and met beautiful Orehu on a glistening northern beach. Orehu had showed him how to cleanse his wounds, shown him special places to bathe, had taken care of him until he was whole again and had set off on his way home.

When Guagugiona arrived home, he found a whole new race of women had replaced those he had taken away. Only the sons of the men he had left were alive and they were old men when he returned. They told him how the men, desperate for the company of women, had encountered some strange wooden people in the forest. They were neither male nor female and after many attempts they captured some along with a wood pecker. The woodpecker had then pecked holes in the people and made them women.

Tamusi thought of his mother. It was true his mother was, like most of the women in the town, not of the same people as his father; the women spoke a different language too, but he had always understood that they were captured in wars with other peoples, not descendants of wooden people, fashioned as it were by man for his own use. This had always puzzled him, how his mother, such a human person (sometimes he thought, more human than his father's people) could have come from a wooden people. Who knows what was true, now, away from all those familiar things, alone, now his father was but spirit? Anything could be true, myth, legend, "real life", all merged on the open, ever-changing sea, where every stroke with his paddle seemed to be another drop of water filling his life with sea, filling the space between himself and home, filling his world with uncertainty.

Leaving home, he felt like he was dying or close to death. The thought of the awesome journey ahead made him feel that he was living on borrowed time, that if he lived it would be a new life.

Cut off from what he had known all his life and venturing into a world he knew only through the mouths of storytellers, he knew that survival was a moment by moment, a day by night affair.

OTHER BOGLE-L'OUVERTURE PUBLICATIONS

Poetry
Dread Beat and Blood by Linton Kwesi Johnson
(third reprint)
Ammunition by Sam Greenlee
At School Today by Accabre Huntley

Children's Books
Rain Falling, Sun Shining by Odette Thomas
Getting to Know Ourselves by Phillis and Bernard Coard
Joey Tyson by Andrew Salkey
Annancy's Day at Cricket by Faustin Charles
Danny Jones by Andrew Salkey
The River That Disappeared by Andrew Salkey

Economics
Minerals in African Underdevelopment by Samuel Ochola

Short Stories
Annancy's Score by Andrew Salkey

Anthologies
Writing in Cuba Since the Revolution edited by Andrew Salkey
One Love edited by Audvil King et. al

History
The Groundings with My Brothers by Walter Rodney
How Europe Underdeveloped Africa by Walter Rodney
Bogle-L'Ouverture Publications Limited celebrates its tenth
anniversary (1969-1979) with the following forthcoming titles :

Novel
Countryman Karl Black by Neville Farki

Religion
The Complete Rastafari Bible with an overview by Robert A. Hill

Bogle-L'Ouverture Publications—
Series No. 7